Electronic Legal Research
An Integrated Approach
Second Edition

Electronic Legal Research
An Integrated Approach
Second Edition

STEPHANIE DELANEY, JD

DELMAR
CENGAGE Learning

Australia • Brazil • Japan • Korea • Mexico • Singapore • Spain • United Kingdom • United States

DELMAR
CENGAGE Learning™

Electronic Legal Research: An Integrated Approach, Second Edition
Stephanie Delaney, JD

Vice President, Career and Professional Editorial: Dave Garza

Director of Learning Solutions: Sandy Clark

Acquisitions Editor: Shelley Esposito

Managing Editor: Larry Main

Product Manager: Melissa Riveglia

Editorial Assistant: Lyss Zaza

Vice President, Career and Professional Marketing: Jennifer McAvey

Marketing Director: Debbie Yarnell

Marketing Manager: Erin Brennan

Marketing Coordinator: Jonathan Sheehan

Production Director: Wendy Troeger

Production Manager: Mark Bernard

Senior Content Project Manager: Kathryn B. Kucharek

Art Director: Joy Kocsis

Technology Project Manager: Tom Smith

Production Technology Analyst: Thomas Stover

For product information and technology assistance, contact us at
Professional & Career Group Customer Support, 1-800-648-7450

For permission to use material from this text or product, submit all requests online at **cengage.com/permissions**
Further permissions questions can be e-mailed to
permissionrequest@cengage.com

Library of Congress Control Number: 2008926709

ISBN-13: 978-1-4180-8088-4

ISBN-10: 1-4180-8088-8

Delmar
5 Maxwell Drive
Clifton Park, NY 12065-2919
USA

Cengage Learning products are represented in Canada by Nelson Education, Ltd.

For your lifelong learning solutions, visit **delmar.cengage.com**

Visit our corporate website at **cengage.com**

NOTICE TO THE READER

Publisher does not warrant or guarantee any of the products described herein or perform any independent analysis in connection with any of the product information contained herein. Publisher does not assume, and expressly disclaims, any obligation to obtain and include information other than that provided to it by the manufacturer. The reader is expressly warned to consider and adopt all safety precautions that might be indicated by the activities described herein and to avoid all potential hazards. By following the instructions contained herein, the reader willingly assumes all risks in connection with such instructions. The reader is notified that this text is an educational tool, not a practice book. Since the law in constant change, no rule or statement of law in this book should be relied upon for any service to any client. The reader should always refer to standard legal sources for the current rule or law. If legal advice or other expert assistance is required, the services of the appropriate professional should be sought.

The Publisher makes no representations or warranties of any kind, including but not limited to, the warranties of fitness for particular purpose or merchantability, nor are any such representations implied with respect to the material set forth herein, and the publisher takes no responsibility with respect to such material. The publisher shall not be liable for any special, consequential, or exemplary damages resulting, in whole or part, from the readers' use of, or reliance upon, this material.

Printed in the United States of America
3 4 5 6 7 12 11

This book is dedicated

to Gavin Smith.

Contents

Preface

"Give a person a fish and they eat for a day, Teach a person to fish and they eat for a lifetime."

Ancient Chinese Proverb

As the power and convenience of electronic legal research continues to penetrate the legal world, schools scramble to train students to use the newest research tools. The few textbooks that touch on this subject seem to spoon-feed students information: "Here's how to log on to Westlaw." "This is a good Internet site for researching statutes." In essence, those texts give students fish. This text is different. For law and paralegal students, lawyers, paralegals, legal secretaries, or anyone wanting to learn more about legal research, *Electronic Legal Research: An Integrated Approach* explains the how and the why of legal research. It fully explains rationale of putting together a query and guides readers through the steps to determine their own best sites for researching statutes. *Electronic Legal Research: An Integrated Approach* teaches readers to fish the changing seas of electronic legal research. They will be competent to fish for a lifetime.

Electronic Legal Research: An Integrated Approach explores the topic of database searching with substance and depth in order to facilitate long-term learning. However, this text does not attempt to cover every kind of computer-based legal research. New products are introduced every day, and the market leaders constantly change. Rather than try to discuss each database separately, this text takes the approach that one set of skills—Boolean searching—will enable the student researcher to do research in nearly any electronic database. This text teaches those skills, specifically training students to research paid legal databases and the Internet by using methods that they can apply to any other electronic database.

Electronic Legal Research: An Integrated Approach is based on the concept of critical thinking, the process of carefully considering information to determine its veracity and usefulness. In the context of research, critical thinking enables the student to make intelligent decisions about how to find information through effective resource selection and query construction. Rather than a traditional how-to book, *Electronic Legal Research: An Integrated Approach* truly facilitates student learning by presenting comprehensive information and challenging exercises that focus on critical thinking skills and practical skill implementation. The comprehensive, critical thinking approach taken in *Electronic Legal Research: An Integrated Approach* makes the text a useful research guide for both students and working professionals, for both paralegals and attorneys. Current manuals on computer-assisted legal research are segmented, covering only the Internet or just Westlaw or Lexis. *Electronic Legal Research: An Integrated Approach* pulls the resources together and demonstrates how the same set of skills can be applied to most research. In addition, currently available research manuals give information without explaining how that information was arrived at or why the information is valid. *Electronic Legal Research: An Integrated Approach* presents students with the logic behind the information. So when the information becomes outdated (as quickly happens in the electronic world), readers have the skills to find their own way. That makes *Electronic Legal Research: An Integrated Approach* different, and this difference enables readers to maximize their research potential.

WHY I WROTE THIS TEXT

Learning effective research skills can be very difficult. Traditionally, students who excelled in this area often did so through luck or sheer determination. *Electronic Legal Research: An Integrated Approach* aims to level the playing field by providing clear, understandable steps to creating effective searches in nearly any database. It teaches the process of electronic legal research in a user-friendly, accessible tone that invites students to achieve research excellence.

In this information age, legal professionals rely more and more on database information retrieval—not only in legal research, but also in managing litigation documents, client files, and calendaring systems. Skills used for information retrieval are the same skills used for legal research, and this text helps students make that connection. When students do not realize this, each new database can seem intimidating. I wrote this book primarily to share this valuable information and to remove fear and intimidation from legal research and from database searching.

ORGANIZATION OF THE TEXT

Electronic Legal Research: An Integrated Approach uses a completely unique approach to teaching on-line research. Rather than dedicating a chapter to Lexis and Westlaw and another to the Internet, the text takes an integrated approach, showing that one research skill can provide success in most research arenas. *Electronic Legal Research: An Integrated Approach* focuses on research strategies and query formation based on Boolean search operators.

Electronic Legal Research: An Integrated Approach shows that Boolean searching is the basis of all electronic research; if students can do an effective Boolean search, they can search for anything anywhere. Through integrated exercises, the student learns that Lexis, Westlaw, and the Internet are not all that different from each other and that the same set of skills leads them to successful results in each arena. Because of that, students develop the flexibility needed to adapt to the quickly changing seas of electronic research.

The text is divided into two parts. Part One (Chapters 1 through 4) explains How to Search. Chapters 1 and 2 explain the basics of searching computer databases using effective queries. These chapters also give students some general query-forming strategies. Chapters 3 and 4 explain how to apply the query strategies to a variety of databases, including Westlaw, Lexis, and the Internet.

Part Two (Chapters 5 through 8) focuses on Where to Search. It applies the strategies of Part One to specific types of legal research, including statutes, regulations, case law, and secondary sources. The idea is to integrate research strategies with the information sources. When this happens, the student can decide effectively where to look for the information she wants and knows exactly how to get it.

Within Chapters 5 through 8 students learn how to use paid legal databases and the Internet to create effective queries. Students learn to efficiently find the information they need using the information they have. Students also learn how to compare the merits of each research resource when more than one is available so that their research process can be effective and efficient.

Most texts that touch on electronic legal research include extensive step-by-step how-to sections on Lexis and Westlaw. This text does not. These products change rapidly. With such constant change in the legal research world, *Electronic Legal Research: An Integrated Approach* relies primarily on the training materials that Westlaw, Lexis, and other paid legal databases provide to their subscribers. These materials do an excellent job of covering the basics of how to use their products. This text then provides basic instructions plus a coherent, integrated approach to searching the databases by using the Boolean search strategies.

The text does not include information on Natural Language searching. This is because Natural Language searching is not included in most databases. Once one masters Boolean searching, it is easy to use Natural Language searching and it requires no additional instruction. However, if one primarily learns Natural Language searching, one will be intimidated by databases that lack that feature. This is an outcome that this text hopes to help avoid.

FEATURES OF THE TEXT

- **Encourages critical thinking.** *Electronic Legal Research: An Integrated Approach* applies the critical thinking model of learning. Rather than spoon-feeding the student with popular Web sites and simplistic Westlaw queries, it engages the student with the actual elements of query formation. The student is guided in *how* to learn, not simply told what to learn. This subtle yet significant shift in instruction enables the student to come to his or her own learning realizations. Students remember things better when they figure them out themselves.
- **Thought-provoking exercises.** To implement the critical thinking model, each learning section has thought-provoking exercises.
- **Guided Exercises.** These in-depth exercises lead the student through the steps necessary to learn a new skill. Then additional exercises encourage the student to experiment with what he learned.
- **Side notes.** Throughout the text, side notes alert students to common errors and strategies to consider as they research.
- **Exercise worksheets.** Worksheets help the student work through the material in the chapter. They appeal to the visual learner. The worksheets provide an alternative presentation of the information in each chapter in a format that can be immediately applied to learning.

HOW TO USE THIS TEXT

Instructors can use the text in one of two ways. First, the text can be a companion to a current legal research text. Most legal research texts touch lightly on electronic legal research. By using this text with a regular legal research text, instructors can easily integrate electronic legal research into every component of learning. The short chapters and no-nonsense approach make this text an ideal tool for a holistic approach to research.

Electronic Legal Research: An Integrated Approach can also be used as a stand-alone text for an advanced legal research class. (The text does not include enough basic research information for an introductory legal research class.) Experienced legal research students can achieve a new level of skill and comfort with their research abilities. Using the text in this manner also gives the student a chance to reinforce information learned in earlier legal research classes.

Whether used as a companion or stand-alone text, the features of *Electronic Legal Research: An Integrated Approach* facilitate comprehensive learning. Each chapter contains a Guided Exercise to help the student work through research problems logically, using information learned in the text. In later chapters, Guided Exercises also keep the foundation information, learned in Part One, fresh in students' minds. This facilitates comprehensive rather than compartmental learning.

Chapter Review Exercises give students opportunities to implement their learning. Exercise questions require students to incorporate information from earlier chapters, to facilitate a holistic approach to research. In keeping with the critical thinking approach of the text, each exercise question requires actual thought—the student cannot simply copy an answer from the text. This again enforces student learning and empowers students to truly learn valuable research skills.

Worksheets in each chapter give students a visual way to manage and incorporate information learned in the chapter. Many worksheets are useful for several different chapters, helping to reinforce the information learned in earlier chapters and enhancing the comprehensive approach to research.

To facilitate ease of use, exercises and worksheets are available in PDF format on the Online Companion. This feature is intended to encourage students to create their own useful reference notebook. The author has discovered that students appreciate the opportunity to use a binder and create a quick reference notebook to use while researching. Students can compile the completed exercises, and worksheets, and put them in a binder, together with computer printouts, class handouts, and other information they gather on electronic legal research. This notebook of documents provides an easily updatable reference tool that students can use long after they leave the classroom. Both methods give the student an updateable resource that ensures that they will not forget their newly learned skills.

SUPPLEMENTAL MATERIAL

- **Instructor's Manual with Test Bank:** Written by the author of this text and available exclusively online, the Instructor's Manual contains chapter introductions, suggestions for emphasis, and teaching tips. It also includes answers to exercises, along with information on how to find answers, and ideas on crafting additional exercises. This manual should prove useful to instructors who are themselves learning to master electronic research. The Instructor's Manual can be found online at (**http://www.paralegal.delmar.cengage.com**).
- **Online Companion™.** The Online Companion™ includes text updates and information to keep students current with the regularly changing world of electronic legal research. The Online Companion™ will also host the same worksheets found in the text, as well as useful links for students and instructors. This information is designed to help the student move from theory to practice. The Online Companion™ can be found at (**http://www.paralegal.delmar.cengage.com**) in the Online Companion™ section of the Web site.

WEB PAGE

Come visit our Web site at (**http://www.paralegal.delmar.cengage.com**), where you will find valuable information such as hot links and sample materials to download, as well as other Delmar Cengage Learning products.

Please note the Internet resources are of a time-sensitive nature and URL addresses may often change or be deleted.

Contact us at (http://www.paralegal.delmar.cengage.com).

For additional resources, please go to http://www.paralegal.delmar.cengage.com

About the Author

Stephanie Delaney is an attorney and educator. She earned her Law degree from the University of San Diego School of Law. She also holds a master's degree in Environmental Law from Vermont Law School and has nearly completed a doctorate in education from the University of Nebraska at Lincoln. She has taught paralegals legal research, both in the classroom and over the Internet, for several years. She is a popular workshop presenter on topics regarding education and technology.

Acknowledgments

Thanks to my ever patient husband Gavin Smith, who supported me in many ways as I worked on the update to this text. I also thank my mother, Winona Delaney, for reviewing every word of my initial text and coming back for more in the second edition. Thanks also to my students who tested out the exercises: Richard Robbins, Amy Keats, Lori King and Ponchie Jones. Thanks to Dr. Joe Mills for the cartoon art. Finally, I would like to thank the following reviewers for their valuable feedback:

Eli Bortman
  Babson College, Wellesley, MA
Joni Boucher
  Sonoma State University, Rohnert Park, CA
Michele Bradford
  Gadsden State Community College, Gadsden, AL
Dora Dye
  City College of San Francisco, San Francisco, CA
James Hightower
  Pensacola, FL
Stonewall Van Wie, III
  Del Mar College, Corpus Christi, TX

Stephanie Delaney

For the Student

HOW TO USE THIS TEXT

Welcome to *Electronic Legal Research: An Integrated Approach*. The purpose of this book is to introduce you to the process of researching law by using electronic (computer-based) sources.

Researching is the process of identifying an issue and then finding relevant information to address that issue. For hundreds of years, this meant scanning through paper indexes to find answers contained in books on library shelves. Though this type of search still has its place and is important, the advent of computers brought us new, faster ways to find answers to questions.

Information traditionally stored in books is now frequently stored in computer databases. The advantage here is that computer databases can be searched in seconds, rather than the hours that a traditional search can take. If you ask the right question, the answer you want will pop up on your computer screen in a fraction of the time needed to find the same information in books.

Of course, every technology has its drawbacks. If you do not ask just the right question, the computer database search can return too much information—hundreds of pages of useless responses with a few lines of good information mixed in. Alternatively, a computer search could bring back too few answers, even when you are confident that more information is out there.

This text shows you how to ask the right questions of the right databases so that you can do effective legal research by using computer resources. This text assumes you have a basic knowledge of how to perform legal research by using books. Indeed, this text might supplement your regular legal research text. Because most electronic versions of legal resources are based on the books that they come from, first understanding how to research using books is essential. If you are unclear on how to do a specific type of research using books, refer to your main legal research text.

This text begins with Part One, which explains how to search. Chapters 1 and 2 explain the basics of searching computer databases by using effective search questions, or *queries*. These chapters also give you some general query-forming strategies. Chapters 3 and 4 explain how to apply the query strategies to a variety of databases, including Westlaw, Lexis, and the Internet.

Part Two applies the strategies of Part One to specific types of legal research, including statutes, regulations, case law, and secondary sources. The idea is to integrate research strategies with research tools. When this happens, you can decide effectively where to look for the information you want and know exactly how to get it.

Both Parts One and Two include helpful charts and worksheets to make organizing your research easier. Several worksheets are duplicated in different chapters so that you can fill in the information specific to the current chapter. You can also find printable versions of the worksheets on the Online Companion, the Web supplement to this text.

This text takes a critical thinking approach to learning. What this means to you is that the book does not give you all the answers. Rather, this text strives to give you the information you need to come up with your own answers. For instance, instead of telling you that a certain Web site is the best for legal research, this text tells you what elements make a good Web site and lets you draw your own intelligent conclusions.

Each chapter has a Guided Exercise that takes you through the process of solving a research process step by step. These exercises help you figure out how to really do the problems and to identify typical mistakes. When going through the chapter, do not just read the Guided Exercise; work it through at your computer—do each step. If you run into trouble, write your questions and take them to your instructor. This helps you learn the material more quickly and easily.

An Online Companion supplements this text. The Online Companion has links to information referenced in the chapters, as well as additional exercises for extra help if information does not make sense the first time around. The field of electronic legal research is changing rapidly, and the Web site is designed to help you keep current.

Each chapter of the text builds on previous sections, providing you with an integrated approach to database searching. When you finish the text, you should have the confidence to search any electronic database with success.

How to Search

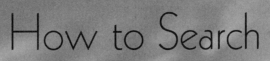

PART

I

Basic Electronic Searching

CHAPTER OBJECTIVES

- **Learn general concepts of using electronic tools:** Using electronic tools to do legal research is not as hard as you might think.
- **Understand Boolean searching:** Boolean logic underlies almost every database of legal information. When you understand how it works, you'll realize that all electronic searching is the same.
- **Use Boolean operators:** Three short words—*AND, NOT,* and *OR*—are the cornerstones of electronic research.
- **Use other operators:** Proximity and phrase searches and wildcard operators can narrow or expand basic searches, enabling you to craft more concise queries.

ON THE WEB

- http://www.paralegal.delmar.cengage.com
- Annotated Web links leading you to:
  - Information on George Boole
  - More information on Boolean operators
- Exercises for additional help

ELECTRONIC LEGAL RESEARCH

research
looking through information to find the answer to a question.

Research is the process of looking through information to find the answer to a question. When you first learn to do traditional legal research, you typically learn various skills separately. You learn to research using digests, popular names tables, or keyword indexes. Over time, you realize what makes legal research complicated: Most sources require slightly different searching strategies.

electronic research
looking for answers to questions by using computer databases of information.

Electronic research is similar, except that you look for answers in computer databases. You generally learn to use resources such as Lexis or Westlaw or Loislaw. You realize that research using the electronic sources is, like using traditional resources, complicated by differences between sources. You may learn to use one form of electronic legal research really well and then avoid research tools that you did not learn in school.

You do not need to work that way. In fact, you may be surprised to learn that electronic searching is basically the same from product to product. One factor that unifies electronic searching is the method of searching known as Boolean searching. Once you focus on similarities rather than the differences, electronic legal research suddenly becomes much easier.

OVERVIEW OF BOOLEAN SEARCHING

database
organized collection of information, searchable by keyword.

Boolean searching is based on the logical structures of algebra first put together by a British man named George Boole in 1847.[1] But, do not let its math basis scare you; Boolean searching is pretty simple to understand. When you search for information electronically, you are generally searching for information stored in some kind of **database**, an organized collection of information. You want to search the database and pull out the individual items relevant to your needs. The logic of Boolean searching lets you do that.

BASIC BOOLEAN OPERATORS

Boolean operator
special word used to connect search terms when searching a database.

connector
see Boolean operator.

You form Boolean search queries by using basic words—*AND, OR, NOT*—to determine whether a query, or question, is true or false. Using those simple words, known as **Boolean operators** or **connectors**, you can join search terms in ways that let you to search the database and find the documents that you want. For example, suppose you are curious about recalls of toys distributed by fast-food restaurants. You remember that, several years ago, the fast-food chain Burger King gave out Pokéballs with its kids' meals.[2] After a short time, the company found that the toys were dangerous for children under three and recalled the toys. You determine that product liability is an issue here, and you want more information. (Chapter 2 describes how to identify an issue if you do not know the relevant area of law.)

To find the information, you can use the Boolean search operators to work in a basic query.

OR

The most basic Boolean search operator is OR. Many search tools default to OR. The **default operator** is the Boolean operator search tools automatically use when a query contains words without connectors between them. You should always check the Help section to see what the default operator is.

Using OR to begin your product liability search, you could create a query that looks like this:

Product OR liability

A search tool answers a query like this in three steps:

1. It looks for every document containing the word *product*.
2. It looks for every document containing the word *liability*.
3. It presents you with a list of all these documents.

The results of this search should be documents on product liability. However, the results might also include contract documents on *product* warranties or environmental cases on strict *liability*. As you can see, you might waste a lot of time reviewing irrelevant results.

default operator
Boolean operator (usually OR) that a database automatically chooses when no Boolean operator is selected.

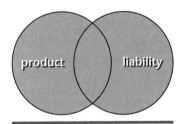

Exhibit 1–1 Venn diagram illustrating how the Boolean operator OR works.

AND

When you search, you generally want all words in your query to appear in the search results. To make that happen, use the popular AND operator. In our product liability search, a query using AND might look like this:

Product AND liability

A search tool answers a query by using these terms in three steps:

1. It looks for every document containing the word *product*.
2. It looks for every document containing the word *liability*.
3. It presents you with documents that contain both *product* and *liability*.

The results of that query are much better than the results of the OR query. However, the results might still include lots of documents that you do not want.

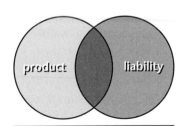

Exhibit 1–2 Venn diagram illustrating how AND works. The darkest shaded area indicates the results.

Imagine that your search brings you dozens of documents on silicone breast implants, which have been the subject of quite a bit of product liability litigation. However, because you are not interested in that topic, you want to omit these documents from the results. This is the perfect opportunity to use the NOT operator.

NOT

The NOT operator is a great way to exclude documents you know will be irrelevant. So, you could try a search like this:

Product AND liability NOT implant

To conduct this search, a search tool performs four steps:

1. It looks for every document containing the word *product*.
2. It looks for every document containing the word *liability*.
3. It selects documents containing both the words *product* and *liability*.
4. It omits documents containing the word *implant* when it presents the results.

You do not always know which documents to omit before you start your search. However, if you start a search and then see a pattern in the irrelevant documents retrieved, you can use the handy NOT operator to modify your search and narrow your results. Note that you do not need to omit the entire phrase *silicone breast implant*, because the words generally come together as a phrase. You could use any of the three words in your NOT query to get similar results.

The basic Boolean search operators are the cornerstones of every electronic database, legal or non-legal. A clear understanding of these operators dramatically improves your research effectiveness.

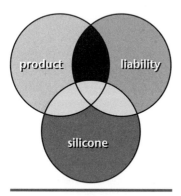

Exhibit 1–3 Venn diagram illustrating how NOT works. The darkest shaded area indicates the results.

Guided Exercise

This exercise takes you step by step through the process of forming a basic query using the Boolean operators AND, OR, and NOT. This exercise will introduce you to the process of query formation. Chapter 2 covers query formation in greater detail.

Our client, the City of Nearwater, wants to build a boardwalk along the seaside to promote tourism in its waterfront area. Nearwater purchased nearly every lot it needs to complete the project, but one homeowner refuses to sell. Nearwater asks us how it can use its power of eminent domain[3] to acquire the property.

keyword
term selected to find relevant documents in a database.

1. **Select keywords.** The first step in our query-forming process is to identify **keywords**, those words that help you to find the answer to your question. When selecting keywords, you want to try to (a) identify major legal themes and (b) identify

specific information to narrow the search. In our example, the major legal theme is eminent domain. For a more specific search term, we might want to use a word related to water, because this action is taking place near the water.

2. **Select Boolean search operators.** After you choose your keywords, you need to join them using Boolean search operators. In our example, we might want to try *eminent* AND *domain* AND *waterfront* OR *seaside*.

In this example, we could build the query without the OR operator and obtain results. However, including common alternative words will broaden our search and let us see whether one word is used rather than the other in the legal context. If your search is not producing satisfactory results, using alternative search terms and the OR operator can help you progress.

You may wonder what would happen if you did not use Boolean operators in your search. Depending on the search tool that you are using, it might have little impact. The tool will automatically insert the default operator into your search and this may give you the results you want. Alternatively, it may give you several hundred irrelevant hits. You can prevent that from happening by always using Boolean operators in your query.

Read the following scenarios. Identify keywords and then try to join the keywords by using Boolean search operators. You do not need to create perfect queries at this point. However, be sure to save your queries—you'll use them again in Exercise 1-2.

**Exercise
1-1**

1. Dick wrote and published a truthful editorial about Jane's bad housekeeping. Jane wants to sue for slander. Can Jane succeed?
2. Lars sold stock for a company that did not exist. Is he liable for fraud?
3. Henry delivered the fresh flowers a day late for Susan's wedding. She had a contract that specified the delivery date, and time was of the essence. What kind of damages could Susan collect for the breach of contact?
4. Zora died and left her entire estate to her cat, Mr. Pipo. Was the will valid?
5. Badco regularly refused to hire female workers over age 24. Is Badco liable for sex discrimination?

OTHER USEFUL OPERATORS

You learned about the basic search operators AND, OR, and NOT. These operators are the foundation of your search. This section introduces other Boolean search terms that will make your search more targeted and accurate.

Proximity Searching

As you learned from the product liability search in the previous section, you could easily do a search resulting in documents where the word *product* appeared on one page and the word *liability* appeared 10 pages later in a different context. To avoid such results, do a **proximity search**. A proximity search, often indicated with the search operator **NEAR**,

proximity search

searching a database for search terms close to each other, usually within 10 to 25 words of each other. This is often indicated with the Boolean operator NEAR.

requires that your search terms be relatively close together, usually within 10 to 25 words of each other. Each search tool has its own default number for proximity. You can determine the default number by looking at the Help section of the database. Using NEAR can really improve the relevance of your search results by increasing the likelihood that your search terms appear as you expect them to.

HELP!

Every search tool has a Help section. Some Help sections are better than others, but you should always read the Help section first when you try a new search tool. The Help section orients you to how Boolean operators work in that search tool. The Help section also enables you to find out what the default operator is. It may also give you wonderful tips on how to search that database successfully.

FDA   **U.S. Food and Drug Administration**   U.S. Department of Health and Human Services

FDA Home Page | Search FDA Site | FDA A-Z Index | Contact FDA

FDA Website Search Tips
Powered by Google

Do a Basic Search
Do an Advanced Search

The Basics of FDA Search

To enter a query, just type in a few descriptive words and hit the 'enter' key or click on the Search button. Since Google only returns web pages that contain all the words in your query, refining or narrowing your search is as simple as adding more words to the search terms you have already entered. Your new query will return a smaller subset of the pages Google found for your original query.

Choosing Search Terms
For best results, it's important to choose your search terms wisely. Keep these tips in mind:

- Try the obvious first. If you're looking for information on Breast Cancer, enter "Breast Cancer" rather than "Cancer".
- Use words likely to appear on a page with the information you want. "LASIK Eye Surgery" gets better results than "what should I expect after LASIK Eye Surgery".
- Make search terms as specific as possible. "ginseng" gets more relevant results than "dietary supplements".

Automatic "and" Queries
By default, Google only returns pages that include all of your search terms. There is no need to include "and" between terms. Keep in mind that the order in which the terms are typed will affect the search results. To restrict a search further, just include more terms.

Automatic Exclusion of Common Words
Google ignores common words and characters such as "where" and "how", as well as certain single digits and single letters, because they tend to slow down your search without improving the results. Google will indicate if a common word has been excluded by displaying details on the results page below the search box.

If a common word is essential to getting the results you want, you can include it by putting a "+" sign in front of it. (Be sure to include a space before the "+" sign.) The one exception to this is "the", which is so common it is not considered in searches.

Google searches are NOT case sensitive. All letters, regardless of how you type them, will be understood as lower case. For example, searches for "breast cancer", "Breast Cancer", and "bReaSt CaNcEr" will all return the same results.

Word Variations (Stemming)
To provide the most accurate results, Google does not use "stemming" or support "wildcard" searches. In other words, Google searches for exactly the words that you enter in the search box. Searching for "consum" or "consum*" will not yield "consumer" or "consuming".

FDA Home Page | Search FDA Site | FDA A-Z Index | Contact FDA | Privacy | Accessibility

FDA Website Management Staff

Exhibit 1–4 FDA Help. Most search engines have sections on how to use them efficiently. From (**http://www.fda.gov**).

Proximity searching does not guarantee that phrases such as *product liability* would appear in the context you want. However, if you are looking for documents about fast-food toy recalls, use proximity searching to improve your results. Here are some examples of possible queries:

Product NEAR liability
Liability NEAR toy

These proximity searches could increase the likelihood that your query will return relevant responses.

Some search tools also enable you to conduct proximity searching with the operator **/n**. The /n directs the search tool to find your words within a certain number (n) of words of each other. To improve your results for our product liability query, you might try:

Product /5 liability

This query requires that the word *product* occur within five words of the word *liability*. The *n* signifies the number of words you want for the proximity.

Phrase Searching

With our fast-food toy scenario, finding the words *product* and *liability* right next to each other would really be useful. A **phrase search** lets you find two or more consecutive words. For phrase searching, most databases require that you use quotation marks or parentheses around the phrase like this:

phrase search
searching a database for an exact phrase, with the search terms right next to each other. Quotation marks or parentheses often surround the phrase.

"product liability"
(product liability)

Phrase searching brings results with the words next to each other. Most search tools find the words in the order presented, though some find the words in any order. Also, phrase searching generally finds plural words (*products, liabilities*). However, it ignores what researchers call **stopwords** (*a, the, to, of, as,* and the like). So a phrase search of *product liability* might find any of the following sentences:

stopwords
words that search tools ignore because they appear too frequently. Examples include the words *the, of,* and *a.*

The court found the plaintiff's distress to be the **product** *of the* **liability** *she bore due to her negligence.*

In a **product liability** *case, the court looks to see whether the manufacturer meets the basic tort elements of negligence.*

If the plaintiff contests liability, the product may stay on the market for many years.

The search ignores stopwords *of* and *the.*

Stopwords

When executing a search, most search tools ignore stopwords. Because they occur so frequently, they would slow the search or give irrelevant results. Listed in the Help section of many search tools, stopwords generally include the following:

- **Articles:** *a*, *an*, *the*
- **Pronouns:** *his*, *her*, *their*
- **Adjectives:** *very*, *many*, *best*
- **Prepositions:** *of*, *in*, *at*
- **Boolean search operators:** AND, OR, NOT, NEAR

The existence of stopwords can pose problems at times. For example, if you search for information on Vitamin A, most search tools only find the word *vitamin*, because A is a stopword. Even if you search for the phrase *Vitamin A*, the search tool ignores the letter A. You might be able to work around that limitation by using words commonly associated with your word or phrase. For example, liver and milk are good sources of Vitamin A. Try this search:

> Vitamin NEAR milk OR liver

Phrase searching may present a danger that can sabotage the unwary researcher's work. It is possible to make your search too specific, so you must be very careful what you ask for in a phrase search query. Recall our fast-food toy recall scenario. If you want to find documents about the Burger King Pokéball case, you might search for a phrase such as

> "Product liability for Burger King Pokéballs".

This query results only in sentences that include our exact phrase. It finds only sentences that contain all the phrase words right next to each other. Thus, a document with a sentence such as this:

> *"The court found that the product liability for the toys rested with the product manufacturer."*

might not appear as a query result, because the words *Burger King* and *Pokéball* are not present. This sentence is very relevant to our search, yet it would not appear in our search results. As you can see, overly specific phrase searching might eliminate perfectly valid results. Phrase searching is a wonderful and valuable tool, but be sure to use it with caution. The next chapter includes more about search strategies.

Wildcard Operators

Searching a database is a fairly precise activity. As you may have experienced, search tools look for exactly what you ask for, misspellings and all.

If you are not sure how to spell a word or if the word has several forms (like *liability* or *liable*), you can use wildcard operators to look for alternatives. The **wildcard operator** lets you use the root of the word to find any words with that root. A wildcard operator is most commonly represented by an exclamation point (!). However, some search tools use a question mark (?) or asterisk (*) to represent the wildcard operator. Wildcard operators, also known as root expanders, are shown in the following examples:

> Liab!
> Child!

The first example finds both the words *liability* and *liable*. The second finds the words *child, children, childish, childlike,* and so on.

Search tools often assume that you want the most common variations of your search terms to appear in your results. This process is known as stemming. **Stemming** is basically the automatic inclusion of a wildcard operator. For example, if you enter the word *ball*, stemming automatically looks for the word *balls*. Many databases perform stemming automatically, eliminating the need to include special operators or additional search operators. However, unlike the wildcard operators, stemming looks only for the most common variations of a word, generally its plural form. To find other forms of the word, like the word *childlike* above, use the wildcard operators. Take a quick look at the Help section of your database to learn whether stemming happens automatically and if so, what kind of stemming the search tool performs.

If your search tool offers stemming and also allows wildcard operators, you can use the two together or separately to obtain the results you want. If you are looking for just the plural of your word, use stemming alone. If you are looking for more complex variations of your word, like *childlike,* use the wildcard operator.

In addition to using a wildcard operator to replace word endings, you can use a wildcard operator to replace specific letters within a word. Often represented by an asterisk or question mark, this wildcard operator can come in handy when you are uncertain of a spelling or when you want to include several variations of the word. For example:

> Wom*n

finds documents containing the words *woman, women, womyn,* and so on. Many databases let you use more than one wildcard at a time. For example:

> *ffect!

finds the words *affect, effect, effecting, affection,* and so on. Using wildcard operators is a great way to increase the scope of your search.

Exercise 1-2

Rewrite your queries from Exercise 1-1, adding phrase searching, proximity searching, and wildcard operators.

SUMMARY

Now you know about the basic tools that many databases use to facilitate your search for information. Whether you use Westlaw or Lexis, an Internet search tool like Google (**http://www.google.com**), or a court records database, you will use some combination of these tools:

- **Boolean operators:** AND, OR, NOT
- **proximity search:** NEAR, /n
- **phrase search:** quotation marks or parentheses
- **word variations:** wildcard operators like asterisk (*), exclamation point (!), or question mark (?); also automatic stemming

Throughout this text, we will explore different databases. As we do, we will first explore how each database uses these operators. As you encounter new databases in your research, whether it is legal research or not, you can make the process of searching much easier if you look in Help and spend a few moments reviewing how each database uses these simple and constant tools.

NOTES

1. Information on George Boole gathered from (**http://www. britannica.com**).
2. "CPSC, Burger King Corporation Announce Voluntary Recall of Pokemon Ball," December 27, 1999. (**https://www.cpsc.gov/ cpscpub/prerel/prhtml00/00046.html**).
3. Eminent domain is the power of a government entity to acquire private property for a public purpose. The government must pay the landowner fair value for the property.

EXERCISES

Chapter Review Exercises

The focus of these exercises is to practice query formation. Read the following questions. Identify the keywords and join them using the search operators explained in this chapter.

1. MeanCredit, Inc. regularly threatens relatives of people who have not paid their bills. Is the company liable for intentional infliction of emotional distress?

2. Alex's cat regularly enters Josh's yard to use the garden as a litter box. Josh is mad and wants to sue Alex. Is Alex liable for the tort of trespass?

3. Last month, Brad failed to pay rent for his apartment. Instead, he used the rent money to make needed repairs to the apartment. Maria, his landlady, has threatened to evict Brad, but he claims the law is on his side, because without the repairs, the apartment is unsafe. Can Maria legally evict Brad?

4. Listening to the radio, Melody, a songwriter, heard a famous pop star singing one of her songs. Melody looked into it and discovered that Off Note Records found her song on the Internet and used the song without her permission. Can Melody sue for copyright infringement?

5. Mohammed, a Muslim, was selected to give the opening prayer next month at the beginning of a football game sponsored by his public school. He wants to say a Muslim prayer, noting that the school permits Christian students to offer their prayers before football games. The school tells Mohammed that he must choose a Christian prayer. He wonders what his rights are under the Freedom of Religion clause of the United States Constitution.

Boolean Search Operators

Operator Type	Terms
Basic Boolean Operators	**AND**–All connected terms appear in each document.
	NOT–Connected term does not appear in the document.
	OR–At least one connected term appears in the document.
Proximity Search	**NEAR**–Connected terms appear within a certain number of words of each other.
	/n–Connected term appears within the specified number (n) of words of each other.
Phrase Search	**Quotation marks** " "–All terms within the marks appear together in the document.
	Parentheses ( )–All terms within the marks appear together in the document.
Word Variations (wildcard)	**Asterisk ***–Depending on the database, substitutes for a letter or series of letters in the term.
	Exclamation point !–Depending on the database, substitutes for a letter or series of letters in the term.
	Question mark ?–Depending on the database, substitutes for a letter or series of letters in the term.

Query Formation
Strategy

CHAPTER 2

CHAPTER OBJECTIVES

- **Query formation strategy:** You are asked to go and find a document—but how do you do it? What keywords should you use, and how should you put them together? In this chapter, you learn the answers to these questions.

- **The five questions:** This simple research strategy helps you form effective queries to get the results you want every time.

- **Troubleshoot queries:** Not finding what you want? You learn how to get your search back on track.

ON THE WEB

- http://www.paralegal.delmar.cengage.com
- Annotated links leading you to:
  - More information on query formation
  - More information on search strategies
- Exercises for additional help

INTRODUCTION TO QUERIES

When you do electronic legal research, you actually extract information from computer databases. Fortunately, the process of searching computer databases is more or less the same, regardless of which database you use. This section provides an overview of that process.

query
request to a database for information it contains, using keywords joined by connectors.

To search a computer database, you begin by constructing a query. A **query** is a list of words, or search terms, that tells the computer what you want to find. For example, you might enter the words *product liability* to ask the search tool to find documents on product liability. However, as we saw in Chapter 1, such searches might find several documents about products, dozens of documents about liability, and only a few documents that actually discuss product liability.

Therefore, to create a good query, you must be more specific. Computer databases provide methods for being specific via the Boolean search operators. As discussed in Chapter 1, a Boolean search operator is just a word, such as *AND, OR,* or *NOT,* that tells the computer database how you want the query to link your search terms. Do you want documents containing the words *product* OR *liability,* or just documents containing the words *product* AND *liability?*

Boolean search operators are key players in building a good query. Often people find mastering the art of crafting the perfect query to be very difficult. Many users become discouraged with their inability to create a good query and thus feel constantly frustrated when trying to search for information.

natural language searching
ability to query a database in the same way that you question a person, without using Boolean operators.

To overcome this frustration, many databases have what is known as natural language searching. **Natural language searching** lets you ask the database your question in the same way that you would ask a person, without using the rather unnatural Boolean search operators. For example, you might ask:

> Is Burger King liable for harm suffered by children who used the Pokéball?

Behind the scenes, the natural language program in the database analyzes your question, translating it into a Boolean search. The translated query might look like this:

> "Burger King" /5 liable AND /5 harm AND children OR Pokéball

The database runs the translated Boolean search, and you do not have to select Boolean operators. On the surface, natural language searching is a straightforward and easy option. However, you will soon find that natural language searches are not as targeted as Boolean searches that you create yourself; they can yield a significant number of irrelevant results. That is because the natural language program is guessing what you want to find, and it sometimes guesses wrong.

Thus, this chapter and the text as a whole focuses on Boolean searching. There are a few reasons for this. First, skilled Boolean searching has been and is likely to continue to be the most efficient method of searching. In addition, Boolean searching is appropriate for nearly every kind of database. Once you become comfortable with Boolean searching, you can easily search most databases. On the other hand, few databases can perform natural language searching. Finally, if a natural language search feature is available, you can always start there. If your natural language search is not successful, you have your Boolean skills to fall back on. However, if you never master Boolean searching, you have nothing to fall back on. So this chapter focuses on building those skills necessary to craft a universally good query using Boolean search operators.

First, you need a strategy. You might find this initial step of legal research hard to remember, because when you have something to research, you want to get right to it. You long to go straight to the books or to log onto Lexis or Westlaw quickly and start searching. However, you will immediately benefit from taking your time and creating a well crafted query. A few minutes spent thinking about what you want to find and where to find it is time well spent. Students are frequently frustrated because they are not sure where to start a legal research project. The query formation strategy should take care of that, helping you know where to begin and how to move forward.

This text emphasizes the use of a **research strategy**, a plan that makes you think about the task ahead. A research strategy is important in facilitating an effective research process. Forming a good query without it is difficult. The research strategy might seem a bit cumbersome at first, but this planning process soon becomes second nature. Also, keep in mind that the same strategy works for every kind of research, legal or non-legal, with computers or with books.

research strategy
plan created to make the researcher think about the research to be done, which thus makes the process more effective. The plan usually includes a determination of relevant law and the best keywords.

A QUERY FORMATION STRATEGY

You can use any strategy that works for you; the one presented here works well for many students. Once you have a question that you need to research, ask yourself the following **Five Questions** to find potential answers.

Five Questions
a research strategy.

> **Question 1: What is the general legal topic?**
> **Question 2: What type of law am I looking for?**
> **Question 3: What secondary sources do I investigate?**

Question 4: What specific source will I select to find the information?
Question 5: How do I formulate my query?

The next sections discuss each of the Five Questions individually.

Question 1: What is the general legal topic?

Most legal questions fall under one or more topics of law. Therefore, answering this first question relies a great deal on your basic knowledge of the law. If you look at a question and have absolutely no idea what area of law it is, follow these very general guidelines about some major categories of law. Keep in mind that your issues may involve more than one area of law.

- **Civil or criminal:** Is someone trying to sue someone else? If so, you know the area of law is civil, not criminal. If the state is prosecuting someone, the issue is a criminal one.

- **Criminal law:** Is someone facing jail time? Was a crime committed? Is a prosecutor involved? Is the government the plaintiff? Are police involved? If so, you are looking at a criminal law issue.

- **Civil procedures:** Some issues fall outside the area of substantive law and concern the legal procedures of court. Is there a question about discovery? About the method or timing of documents filed? If you have a civil procedure issue, remember to refer to the appropriate procedural statute or court rules for more information.

- **Contracts:** Was there an express (written or spoken) agreement between the parties? If so, the issue is probably one of contract law. If the two parties are businesses, the issue may be one of commercial law involving the Uniform Commercial Code.

- **Property:** The several categories of property include real, personal, and intellectual property.

  - **Real property:** Does the question regard the transfer of land from one party to another? That is real property law. Does it regard how one uses the land? That may be zoning and land use law. It could also be about environmental law, which, from a property standpoint, deals primarily with soil contamination and other pollution.

  - **Intellectual property:** Issues of copyrights, patents, and trademarks fall within this category. If your issue concerns rights associated with the creation of books, music, Web pages, new inventions, art, symbols, and the like, your issue may involve the area of intellectual property.

- **Torts:** Has one person harmed another in a non-criminal way? Trespass, fraud, mental duress, auto accidents, slips and falls, and

Exhibit 2–1 Protecting Intellectual property is always important. Illustrated by Joe Mills. Reprinted with permission. All rights reserved.

other personal injuries are addressed by tort law. Tort law also includes product liability, where a consumer product harms someone. That is the case in our Pokéball scenario.

- **Family law:** Does the issue involve marriage and divorce? Children's issues such as child custody, child support, and adoption are all within this category as well.

If, after looking at these general guidelines, you still have no idea of the area of law involved, try a dictionary for unfamiliar words or simply ask someone. Once you know the general area of law, you can go to the next question.

Question 2: What type of law am I looking for?

Is this topic covered by state or federal law or both? Would a statute, regulation, or case law discuss it? Perhaps a combination of all three? To answer these questions, you need a good idea of what types of issues state or federal law covers. One student looking for a divorce statute in the United States Code became very frustrated. She could not find any of the laws she expected, because state law, not federal law, covers most family law issues, including divorce. Knowing whether the relevant law is state, federal, or both assists you in searching successfully.

State law generally regulates topics such as criminal law, family law, contracts, estate planning, and property. Federal law regulates topics dealing with federal laws and the U.S. Constitution. Some areas, such as administrative law and environmental law, may go either way, depending on the parties and the subject involved. Look carefully at any government agency involved—is it a state or federal agency? That answer can give you a good indication of whether state or federal law is involved.

Next, you need to determine whether the relevant law is a statute, regulation, court case, or some combination of all these. Note that statutes tend to be broad pronouncements of law, regulations are more detailed, and cases apply facts to the law in specific situations. If you are uncertain what kind of law to search, try looking for relevant cases, because cases often lead you to other relevant law. Keep in mind that very current issues may not have any cases **on point**. Cases take a while to work their way through the system to the appellate level, where most cases must arrive before they are reported. Remember that this question is important in helping you narrow your search. If you are not sure about the kind of law involved, try looking at some secondary sources mentioned in Question 3. They might help you find the answer.

on point
a case that specifically addresses some or all of a particular issue.

Question 3: What secondary sources do I investigate?

A legal researcher has access to hundreds of secondary sources. The challenge is determining where to begin. Often starting with the basics—a legal dictionary or a legal encyclopedia—is best. A quick search of these sources for your key terms or ideas helps you understand what you are researching and gives you a big-picture overview of the topic. It also gives you additional keywords and generally facilitates your research. Hornbooks and practice guides are also useful in getting a good grounding in relevant law. Spending 20 or 30 minutes familiarizing yourself with the area of law you are researching saves lots of time and effort later.

Question 4: What specific source will I select to find the information?

In electronic legal research, you can choose to search a variety of databases. One might have information on federal statutes, another might contain all federal case law, and a third might combine the two kinds of information. In addition, you might have access to several different sources of information, for example, the Internet, Westlaw, and specialized desk books. Deciding which resource or combination of resources to start with is part of a good strategy.

Be specific when answering this question. Rather than generally determining to use the Internet, you should instead brainstorm about

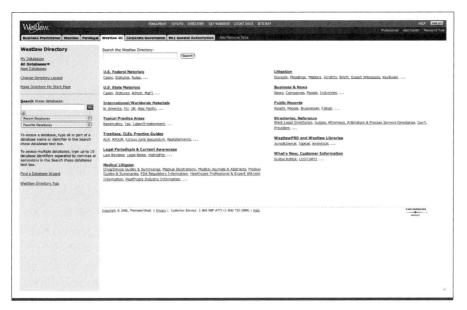

Exhibit 2–2 Westlaw makes selecting the right directory easy. From Westlaw Westmate. Reprinted with permission of Thomson/West. All rights reserved.

which specific Web sites to use or which specific search engine to use to find the Web sites. Rather than simply deciding to use Westlaw, determine which directory and specific file to start in. This step further helps to focus your search and obtain the results you want. If you do not know right away where to start, take a moment to try to think it through. In any case, try to be as specific as possible.

Question 5: How do I formulate my query?

At this point, you begin determining exactly how to ask for the information you want to find. What keywords will you use? How will you put them together? Which combinations of Boolean search operators will yield the best results? Strategizing ahead of time about how to put your query together can help you focus on this most frustrating step of searching.

Keep one important thing in mind: Once you form a query, do not become too attached to it. If you devise a query you like, try it a few times to see what kind of results you get. If you do not get the results you want, do not be afraid to edit the query a little or toss it altogether and try something else.

Answering this query construction question also requires you to focus on your keywords. The first four questions help lead you to keywords, but the actual process of selecting the best keywords is an art that you learn over time. Here are some strategies:

issue statement
legal question that research aims to answer.

- **Put your question into an issue statement.** This works best when you use the whether/when format. For example, in the previous chapter, we wanted to know about Burger King's liability for the Pokéball. An issue question in the whether/when format might read:

  > **Whether** Burger King is liable for injuries caused by the Pokéball **when** it distributed the balls without age appropriate warnings?

  Simply formulating the issue statement helps you organize your thoughts. The first part of the issue statement (whether) focuses on the broader issue, in this case, liability for injury. The second part of the statement (when) focuses on the particular, in this case, distribution of the toys without an appropriate warning. In other words, your question begins a process of analysis in which you combine the legal rule with the important facts of the matter.

- **Avoid overly fact-specific words.** A query for relevant cases on the Burger King matter that includes the words *Burger King* and *Pokéball* would probably produce few results. The same query might work well for fact-specific media searches, but given the more general nature of legal authorities, such words are unlikely to yield successful results. So focus instead on general legal principles, in this case, product liability.

- **Be careful with statutes.** Statutes often use specific legal words with specific legal meanings. For example, in some states, marriages are dissolved. If you search these states' statutory law for the term *divorce*, you would have no luck, because all these statutes use the word *dissolution* instead. If you are uncertain of the specific word the statutes use, try guessing, using a variety of words with the OR operator. (Guessing is a perfectly legitimate search tactic!) If that doesn't work, try a keyword search of cases to see if any refer to the statute. Courts often use the more common words in their decisions, especially in the statement of facts.

The query construction phase of your planning is the time you need to think about which combination of Boolean operators to use. Sometimes simple searches get you where you want to go; more often you will want to combine operators to obtain the best results. If you are looking for a news story on the Pokéball matter, you might try a query such as this:

"Burger King" AND "product liability" NEAR Pokéball

This combination of keywords and Boolean operators starts you on the path to finding the answer to your question. After reviewing the results, you can determine if the query needs editing or if you found what you wanted on your first try.

The art of putting together a query is emphasized throughout this text. It is the primary skill that separates the effective researcher from the ineffective one. Once you master it, you improve your ability to find just what you are looking for and become more comfortable with actually finding it.

Guided Exercises

The following guided exercise leads you through the process of using the Five Questions.

Remember the Pokéball example from Chapter 1? Burger King recalled the small Pokémon balls distributed with its kids' meals after learning that the toys could endanger children under three. Your client wants to sue Burger King for injury her five-year old child suffered because of the Pokémon ball. Can she prevail? Ask the Five Questions to lay the foundation for your search.

Question 1: What is the general legal topic? Answering this question should be simple, because we already discussed product liability as the type of law. Product liability is a section of tort law, which applies to injuries that require compensation. Even if you did not immediately narrow the choice to product liability, you may have guessed that product liability is a tort.

Question 2: What kind of law am I looking for? Generally, tort law is addressed by cases in common law. However, several statutes at both the state and federal levels also address some product liability issues through consumer protection laws. So choosing which way to go could be a toss-up. If, after some thought, you cannot determine the answer to this question (or any of the Five Questions) move ahead to the next question. This research strategy aims to help you in the research process, not stop you before you even get going!

Question 3: What secondary sources do I investigate? Be specific when answering this question. As you try to lay your foundation for understanding the issue, where should you look? Starting with a legal dictionary or a legal encyclopedia is always good, especially if you have trouble answering Questions 1 and 2. After that, think about whether law review articles might cover the subject. Perhaps the general news media is a good source of information. If the matter involves an industry, try industry newsletters or other publications. Be specific here—doing so makes everything else fall into place more easily.

For our Pokéball case, the general media is a good source of specific information about the facts of this case. Law review articles on product liability could yield some good results as well.

Question 4: What specific source will I select to find the information? Questions 1 through 3 are really foundation questions that help you get enough information to move forward. Question 4, however, is a question of strategy. Where do you begin your search? On the Internet? On a paid legal database? If so, which directory and specific file can provide the best information? Perhaps you want to start with a book, such as a dictionary.

In our case, the Pokéball issue received quite a bit of news coverage, so a general Internet search is a good way to get some background information. When you look for law review articles on product liability, try a paid legal database and look in specific directories on product liability or torts.

(*continued*)

Question 5: How do I formulate my query? After you answer this final question, you can start your search. Keep in mind that over the course of your research, you will probably need to use several different queries to find information in the same resource and certainly several different queries to find information in different resources. Because your queries will vary, you may wonder why you should bother to answer this question. Well, the reason is it provides the opportunity to focus. Simply taking a moment to focus on keywords and phrases and to think about Boolean tools allows you the time to formulate an effective query. The process is far more efficient than guessing as you go along.

Do not become too attached to your query! In fact, you probably want to create several alternative queries before beginning your research, especially if you use paid legal databases. If the first query does not work, you can quickly and easily try the next one.

If your query does not work, check to make sure you are looking in the right place. If you are looking in the right place, try one of your alternate queries. Sometimes, modifying Boolean search terms is all you need to do. If you get too many results, try narrowing your results with a date restriction or more specific database.

For the Pokéball case, the sample query discussed earlier in the chapter might work well:

"Burger King" AND "product liability" NEAR Pokéball

This is, of course, just a sample formulation. Depending on the type of database you select, the query may or may not be effective. Indeed, the value of a query depends completely on where you perform the search. You can ask the best question in the world, but if it is in the wrong database, you will not receive useful results.

Query formation is a skill that takes time to acquire. There is no right or wrong way to phrase a query and, unfortunately, no magic formula that always gets you perfect results. Be patient as you learn to form well crafted queries and do not give up. Even the most experienced researchers revise their queries, again and again, before they get the results they want.

QUERY TROUBLESHOOTING

Because query formation is a learned skill, in the beginning you can expect to run into some roadblocks. Do not worry—this is normal. If you do not get the results you want from your query, ask yourself the following questions.

- **Did I plan my strategy?** Researchers who are stymied in the research process have often skipped the planning process and thus are not really sure what they are searching for or where they expect to find it. Taking time to think significantly speeds the research process and increases the accuracy of your results.

- **Limit the dates.** The best search tools permit you to limit your search to documents within certain date ranges. If you are searching for a popular subject, try limiting your results to the current year. If you are looking for a case that you know was decided in the early eighties, try limiting your search to "1979–1986." Each database handles date restrictions differently, so be sure to check the Help section for the proper format.

- **Select a more specific database.** The more specific your database, the fewer results you will get. For example, to search for an Idaho products liability case, you might select a database with all federal and state cases. The search will probably get the results that you want, but you may not be able to find them amongst the irrelevant federal cases. Alternatively, you could try searching a database with information on all states. But this would yield results from Indiana as well as Idaho. The most specific database is one with just Idaho cases. So although all three databases contain the right case, the most specific database makes the right case easier to find.

- **Use phrase or proximity searching.** Take advantage of Boolean tools to limit your search to specific phrases or words close to each other. Searching for

    products AND liability AND Pokéball

produces entirely different results than searching for

    "product liability" NEAR Pokéball.

Using proximity and phrase searching, you can effectively narrow your results to the documents you want.

Using the Five Questions, identify the general legal topic and key terms for the following scenarios:

Exercise 2-1

1. Becky wants to buy a house with Diane. They think they want to buy the house as joint tenants, but they are not entirely sure what it means to own real property in joint tenancy.
2. An adoring fan assaulted Susan Rich, the famous poet.[1] Susan learned who did it and wondered if she had any way to sue the fan under civil tort law, aware that cases like hers are usually criminal matters.
3. Carin had been sick for many months, and her doctor told her she had only a day or two left to live. After the doctor left, Carin gave her prized diamond brooch to her nurse, Marta, who had cared for her for many months. Carin miraculously survived and was soon in perfect health. She asked Marta to return the gift, and Marta refused. Is there anything Carin can do?

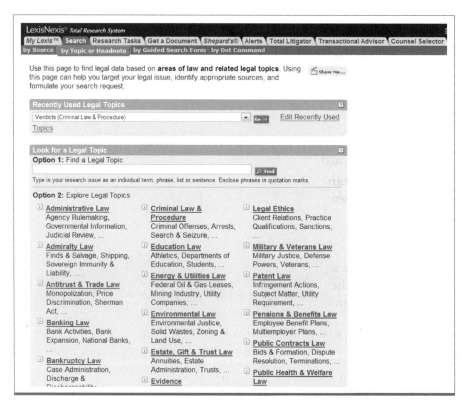

Exhibit 2–3 In most Lexis search screens, you have the option of limiting the date range of your search.

Source: Copyright 2006 LexisNexis, a division of Reed Elsevier Inc. All rights reserved. LexisNexis and the Knowledge Burst logo are registered trademarks of Reed Elsevier Properties Inc. and are used with the permission of LexisNexis.

- **Am I searching in the right place?** The best search query will not yield results from the wrong database. Ask yourself, "Why am I searching this specific database?" If you are not sure, go back to your research strategy. If you began by searching a very specific database, try to broaden your search. If you used restrictions or phrase searching, double-check to make sure you are using these tools correctly. Make sure you are not searching a case database for statutes. If you are searching for statutes, keep in mind that this is one area in which using the right word is essential. Try looking for a statute by finding cases that refer to it, and you can more easily find a statute whose keywords are difficult to determine.

- **Am I using the right words?** Because legal language tends to be obscure, the important task of selecting the correct keywords becomes rather difficult. If you are uncertain of your search terms, consult a legal dictionary or encyclopedia. These valuable secondary sources can help you find the proper phrasing, so you can then find the documents you need. In addition, legal dictionaries and legal encyclopedias often direct researchers to landmark cases that define or explain the word or concept in question. Quickly Shepardizing or cite checking the referenced landmark case can also help put your research on the right track. **Shepardizing**, the process of checking whether a law still applies, can lead you to other cases that reference key sections of the case you search. As a result, you might find even more relevant cases.

- **Do I understand what I am looking for?** Sometimes, you get started on a research project and find just the right case on your first try. Hurray! Unfortunately, if you are not sure what you are looking for, you may find an on point case and not realize it, wasting time as you continue looking for the "right" case. A basic grasp of the area of law you are searching assists you in recognizing valid results when you see them. Refer to a legal dictionary or legal encyclopedia for some background.

- **Am I misusing the phrase operator?** Though phrase searching is a great tool for narrowing results, misusing it can result in no results. Try reworking your query using the NEAR or /n operator to broaden your results.

- **Does what I am looking for exist?** If all attempts fail, you may be looking for something that simply does not exist or is not available electronically. Some things to remember:

  - Most state cases do not make it to the case reporters until the cases reach appellate court. You are not likely to find state cases from the trial court level.

  - Writing and publishing law review and journal articles takes several months. If you search for very current topics (those that arose within the past two to four months), you may not find them addressed in law review articles. Instead, try searching legal and mainstream newspapers or monthly publications.

  - When researching cutting edge areas of law, such as cyberlaw, finding documents that exactly match your issue may be difficult. However, basic legal principles are fairly constant. Thus, if you look for discussions of jurisdiction in cyberspace, traditional cases on jurisdiction can be persuasive, even if they do not specifically focus on cyberlaw.

- **Did I spell my query words correctly?** An otherwise perfectly constructed query containing a simple spelling error can prevent you from getting the results you expect. Such an error can cause frustration, so double-check your spelling.

Sheparding

generally, the process of checking a law to make sure that it still applies. It is also known as "cite checking". When Shepardizing or cite checking cases, you may find other relevant cases that refer to your case, making Shepardizing a good research tool.

Do not become too discouraged when your search does not immediately yield the results you want. Remember that becoming an effective researcher is a process that takes time. Answering these query troubleshooting questions helps you get past many research roadblocks. Use the Query Troubleshooting Worksheet at the end of this chapter as a guide.

SUMMARY

This chapter covers the big topic of how to form an effective query. It looks at a research strategy and explores some troubleshooting questions. Query formation is a learned skill emphasized throughout this book.

Feeling overwhelmed by the task of beginning a new research project is not unusual. Fortunately, using a search strategy can facilitate your task and always give you a place to start. If you take time to use this strategy or another that works well for you, you can perform research faster, more accurately, and with less stress.

NOTE

1. Poet Susan Rich is author of *Cures Include Travel* (2000) and *The Cartographer's Tongue* (2006), both published by White Pine Press.

For additional resources, please go to http://www.paralegal.delmar.cengage.com

EXERCISES

Chapter Review Exercises

Read the following fact scenarios and answer the Five Questions to plan your search process. The handy Five Questions Worksheet at the end of the chapter can assist you. Don't do your search yet—save these answers to perform the searches at the end of Chapter 3, after you have learned more about paid legal databases.

1. Greg and Erich entered into an agreement for Erich to buy a classic guitar from Greg for $950. They had no written agreement; the men just shook hands. Greg told Erich that the guitar would be ready in one week. When Erich arrived at the appointed time to get the guitar, Greg decided he did not want to sell. Erich wants to enforce the agreement. Can he?

2. Doug decided to rob the home of Sally. While in the house, Doug fell on a bicycle in the hall and sprained his ankle. Doug wants to sue Sally for negligence. Can he prevail?

3. After recovering from the sprained ankle, Doug decided to rob a jewelry store. Doug wore a black ski mask but was unarmed. When Doug entered the store, old Mr. Diamond was so horrified that he had a heart attack and died. Can Doug be charged for murder?

4. Javier and Raul bought an old beach house as joint tenants. For many years, the brothers enjoyed the house together. When Javier prepared his will, he left his part of the home to his son Joseph. Is his bequest valid?

5. Ken recently started having stomach problems. He thinks that during surgery five years ago, his doctor left a sponge in his stomach. He wonders if it is too late to sue the doctor for malpractice. Is it?

Worksheet

The Five Questions

A worksheet for initiating research

Question 1: What is the general legal topic?

Hint: Torts? Contracts? Criminal law? Use a dictionary or encyclopedia to get background information and to look up additional keywords.

Answer:

Question 2: What type of law am I looking for?

Hint: State or federal or both? Statute, regulation, case law, or a combination?

Answer:

Question 3: What secondary sources do I investigate?

Hint: Encyclopedia? Law review or journals? Mainstream media? Interest group or agency Web sites?

Answer:

Question 4: What specific source will I select to find the information?

Hint: Answer this question in detail. Do not simply answer the Internet; include possible Web sites. Do not just answer Lexis; include the library and file.

Answer:

Question 5: How do I formulate my query?

Hint: Identify keywords and determine the best way to put them together.

Answer:

Worksheet

Query Troubleshooting

A handy reference for resolving research problems

Troubleshooting Question: Did I plan my strategy?

Comments: Do not skip the planning process! Make sure to complete each step of your strategy.

Result of double checking:

Troubleshooting Question: Am I searching in the right place?

Comments: Make sure that you are using the right database and that the information on it contains is neither too broad nor too narrow for your search.

Result of double checking:

Troubleshooting Question: Am I using the right words?

Comments: Check your terms and include alternative words with the OR operator. Use a legal dictionary to expand possible terms.

Result of double checking:

Troubleshooting Question: Do I understand what I am looking for?

Comments: Make sure you really understand the question. Use a legal dictionary or encyclopedia for clarification.

Result of double checking:

Troubleshooting Question: Am I misusing the phrase operator?

Comments: If using a phrase operator, make sure it is not too specific. Rework using proximity search operators.

Result of double checking:

Troubleshooting Question: Did I spell my words correctly?

Comments: Make sure the spelling, spacing, and punctuation in your search term are correct.

Result of double checking:

Troubleshooting Question: Does what I am looking for exist?

Comments: Think about whether the information exists at all or exists electronically where you are looking.

Result of double checking:

Paid Legal Databases

CHAPTER 3

CHAPTER OBJECTIVES

- **Learn general concepts:** What are paid legal databases? Why do you need them?

- **Explore Westlaw and Lexis:** Everyone in the legal world has heard of these major legal information providers. You will learn to use Boolean search operators in Westlaw and Lexis.

- **Use other paid legal databases:** Loislaw and Casemaker are examples of the many smaller electronic legal databases on the market.

- **Begin your research:** A guided exercise helps you practice using a research strategy in your favorite paid legal database.

ON THE WEB

- http://www.paralegal.delmar.cengage.com
- Annotated links leading you to:
  - Paid legal databases
  - Specific research hints for Westlaw, Lexis, Casemaker, and Loislaw
- Exercises for additional help

paid legal database
legal database that you can access only by
subscribing or paying by the use.

INTRODUCTION

Dozens of **paid legal databases** are on the market today. Everyone recognizes the names *Lexis* and *Westlaw* as the nation's leaders in providing legal information. At the regional level, law offices turn to Loislaw, Fast-Case, Casemaker, and similar products. These products make it possible to access libraries full of books by using only the space of your computer.

New legal databases are introduced frequently and existing products are regularly updated with new features. You could spend a lot of time trying to master each technology individually and become frustrated every time the product is updated or whenever a new product is introduced. However, such frustration is unnecessary. For most research, the same strategies discussed in Chapter 2 will work to get you the results you want: one strategy, many products. So, whether you use Westlaw or Loislaw, you can find what you are looking for with minimal expenditure of time and effort.

Please note that this chapter on paid legal databases does not attempt to teach you how to use individual databases. The information providers have excellent training resources of their own; there is no need to reinvent the wheel. Indeed, many information providers offer online tutorials that teach you the basics and introduce the latest innovations.[1] So, rather than teaching you the nuts and bolts of using the databases, this chapter focuses on how to use the strategies introduced in Chapter 2 to work successfully within each database.

WESTLAW

Westlaw provides access to an extensive library of legal materials. Its primary source databases include cases, statutes, and regulations from all 50 states, the District of Columbia, and several foreign jurisdictions. Westlaw also includes secondary sources such as legal journals, hornbooks, and legal periodicals. In addition, Westlaw provides bill tracking tools (for researching law that has not yet been enacted) and tools to search legislative history (the background of law as it was being created). Westlaw's directories incorporate information from more than 5000 news and business databases.[2] Westlaw offers unique services as well, like the KeyCite citation service, which is similar to Shepard's citation service. KeyCite provides legal history and lists citing references to make sure you have good law.

Westlaw subscribers can access its services through the Internet at Westlaw.com (**http://www.westlaw.com**). This gives the researcher the flexibility to access Westlaw databases from any computer with an Internet connection.

This chapter introduces you to using our research strategies with Westlaw. Later chapters focus on additional searching skills using

Exhibit 3–1 Westlaw logo.
Source: Reprinted with the permission of West Group.

Westlaw. Before doing the exercises in this chapter, you should have a basic familiarity with Westlaw.[3]

Westlaw uses a number of Boolean search features:

- **Boolean operators:** Westlaw uses the Boolean search terms and symbols—AND (&), OR [space], NOT (%), and /n. The default search operator is OR.

- **Proximity search:** There are several options for proximity searching. In addition to the /n operator, you can look for terms in the same sentence (/s, +s) and in the same paragraph (/p, +p).

- **Phrase search:** Westlaw permits phrase searching with quotation marks. For example, you can search for "unauthorized practice of law". Of course, the search ignores the word *of*, because it is a stopword.

- **Stemming:** Westlaw automatically activates the stemming feature, retrieving plurals and possessives of the search terms. You can turn this feature off by putting a # in front of the term.

- **Wildcard:** To perform a wildcard search in Westlaw, use the asterisk (*). For example, *wom*n* retrieves the words *women, woman*, and *womyn*. To find all variations of a word, use an exclamation point (!) at the end of a word.

Westlaw also supports natural language searching. The natural language search enables you to write questions without the use of Boolean search terms, but rather in the language you would naturally use in asking a question. Westlaw's support materials and Help page have more information on its search features.

LEXIS

LexisNexis is another of the original providers of electronic legal research. It provides access to a broad array of information. The Lexis side provides primary and secondary sources of law including legal journals, hornbooks, and legal periodicals. It provides bill tracking tools (for law that has not yet been created) and legislative history tools (for exploring the background of law as it was being enacted). The Nexis side provides non-legal news and information, including access to hundreds of newspapers, trade journals, newsletters, and other information sources.

Most Lexis subscribers access services through the Internet at Lexis.com (**http://www.lexis.com**), so they can use the LexisNexis databases while working on any computer with an Internet connection.

This chapter introduces you to using research strategies in Lexis. Later chapters teach you additional searching skills. Before doing the exercises in this chapter, you should have a basic understanding of Lexis.

Exhibit 3–2 Lexis logo.

Source: From the Lexis-Nexis Web site, (**http://www.lexis.com**). Copyright 2006 LexisNexis, a division of Reed Elsevier Inc. All Rights Reserved. LexisNexis and the Knowledge Burst logo are registered trademarks of Reed Elsevier Properties Inc. and are used with the permission of LexisNexis.

Lexis has three different kinds of searching. The traditional "terms and connectors" search uses Boolean search terms. The natural language search enables you to write questions without the use of Boolean search terms, but rather in the language you would naturally use in asking a question. Finally, Lexis also offers the Easy Search. It is designed to be more "Google-like," allowing quick searches with just a few search terms and combining the best of natural language and Boolean searching. This text will focus on terms and connectors/Boolean searching, because it is the most challenging and the most useful. Your Boolean search skills will enable you to search in any database. However, few databases have natural language or Easy Search features.

Lexis uses the following Boolean search operators in its terms and connectors searching:

- **Boolean operators:** Lexis uses the Boolean search operators AND, OR, NOT, /n, and NOT /n.
- **Proximity search:** In addition to the /n operator, several options are available for proximity searching. You can look for terms in the same sentence (/s) and in the same paragraph (/p).
- **Phrase search:** Lexis permits phrase searching with quotation marks. For example, you can search for the phrase *"unauthorized practice of law."* Of course, the search ignores the word *of*, because it is a stopword.
- **Stemming:** Lexis automatically activates the stemming feature to retrieve plurals and possessives. Lexis also automatically retrieves word equivalents. For example, a search for *wash* returns the words *WA* and *Washington.*
- **Wildcard:** You can perform a wildcard search in Lexis by using the asterisk (*). For example, a search for *wom*n* retrieves the words *women, woman,* and *womyn.* Placed at the end of a word, an exclamation point brings back all variations of that word.

For more information on Boolean search operators in terms and connectors searching, see the Lexis support materials and Help sections.

Exercise 3-1

Form a query from the following issue statements by using the terms and connectors of your favorite paid legal database. After you form the query, select a source and run the search. How many hits did you get? Did you find an answer in the first 10 hits?

1. Whether non-profit organizations can sue when a donor fails to give a promised gift.
   a. query:
   b. source:
   c. hits:

2. Whether an environmental group can buy timber harvest rights when it has no intention of cutting wood.
    a. query:
    b. source:
    c. hits:

3. Whether a person who shares information with a bank for a loan has a right of privacy over personal information.
    a. query:
    b. source:
    c. hits:

4. Whether a nurse would lose her license if she took patient medication for personal use.
    a. query:
    b. source:
    c. hits:

5. Whether a college is liable for cleanup costs when an alum donates a piece of contaminated property.
    a. query:
    b. source:
    c. hits:

OTHER PAID LEGAL DATABASES

Lexis and Westlaw are definitely the market leaders in comprehensive legal research. Their services are like those available at the largest university law libraries, which have extensive collections, including the most obscure law review or treatise. However, space, cost, and convenience also create the need for smaller law libraries—libraries that house information on local statutes and case law, local law reviews, popular practice books, and treatises. Not surprisingly, electronic services have evolved to fill that niche in the electronic legal research world as well. Dozens of companies provide reliable, basic state and federal information for a fraction of the cost of the Lexis and Westlaw services. These types of services are especially attractive to many attorneys who have focused practices and need only limited research materials.

Because dozens of providers offer different local information, addressing them all in this text is impossible. Fortunately, we do not need to. Chapter 1 discussed how all electronic research is basically the same; if you understand how to use one legal database, you can quickly and easily figure out how to use another. Keep that in mind as you read about two representative small legal databases—Loislaw and Casemaker. Each has features that differ from Lexis and Westlaw. The following sections give you a general idea of how to use your basic research skills in these smaller legal databases.

Loislaw

The Loislaw legal database is available to subscribers at (**http://www. loislaw.com**). It has a national scope and contains case law, statutory law, constitutions, administrative law, court rules, and other authority for all 50 states and the District of Columbia, and it includes the decisions of the federal Supreme Court and Court of Appeals. Loislaw also includes a limited selection of secondary sources, including treatises and bar association publications.

Small firms and sole practitioners find small databases like Loislaw useful because they are far less expensive than Westlaw and Lexis. In addition, sometimes finding what you are looking for in a smaller database is easier because there is less to search through.

Although searching Loislaw differs slightly from searching other resources this chapter has explored, it is the same at its core. Here is a list of some notable features:

- **Boolean operators:** Loislaw uses the Boolean operators AND, OR, NOT, and NEAR. It also allows the use of symbols for searching. For example, the ampersand (&) symbol represents AND, and a vertical line (|) represents OR, the default operator. The Loislaw Help section explains all the symbols for the connectors.

- **Proximity search:** Proximity searching is possible using NEAR and specifying the number of words for the proximity search. For example, if you are looking for *battery* within five words of *child*, you would enter *battery NEAR5 child*. If you are doing multiple proximities, use parentheses to help. For example, if you want to find *battery* within five words of *child* and *battery* within five words of *abuse*, you might try this query: *battery NEAR5 (child OR abuse)*. Insiders at Loislaw say that the NEAR operator is their favorite for searching their databases.

- **Phrase search:** You do a phrase search in Loislaw by using quotation marks. For example, you can search for the phrase *unauthorized practice of law*. Of course, the search ignores the word *of*, because it is a stopword.

- **Stemming:** Loislaw automatically looks for the most common variations of single words. For example, if you search for the word *child*, Loislaw also looks for *children*, *childish*, and *childlike*.

Exhibit 3–3 Loislaw logo.

Source: From the Loislaw Web site, (**http://www.loislaw.com**). Used with the permission of Loislaw.

- **Wildcard.** The question mark (?) is a wildcard for single characters within a word or number. For example, a search for *wom?n* finds *women, woman,* and *womyn.* Using the asterisk guides Loislaw to search for all variations of a word or number. For example, if you are uncertain of a date, searching for *199** finds documents created any time during the nineties. Use the asterisk only at the end of a word or number.

Loislaw's support materials and Help page offer more information on searching.

Casemaker

Casemaker is a legal research database that is offered exclusively through state bar associations as a benefit to members. As such, many small- and medium-sized legal offices use this service for the majority of their legal research or as a supplement to the more expensive search tools. Bar association members can access the materials for free, but the materials are not freely available to the public. With no fees associated with each visit or each search, a researcher has the leisure to do complex searching with less stress. Once a search is narrowed enough, one might then go to Lexis or Westlaw and access resources that are not available in smaller tools like Casemaker.

Casemaker's holdings vary by state, but for the most part one has complete access to state constitutions, statutes, regulations, and cases. Casemaker's federal library includes Supreme Court and other federal court decisions, federal statutes, regulations, court rules, and forms. Additionally, one may have access to state court rules, regulatory opinions (including ethics), and local legal journals. Each state works with Casemaker to create a library that will be most useful to the attorneys in the state.

Casemaker is different than the search tools we have explored so far, because it does not use Boolean searching as its base. Rather, it uses a technology called set logic. Fortunately, the strategies you have developed for Boolean searching work for set logic as well. Searching in Casemaker gives you an excellent example of how mastering basic search skills will assist you in searching every kind of database.

You can use Casemaker to do a general search or, when appropriate, you can browse through the **Table of Contents** of statutes, regulations, and court rules. The Table of Contents feature facilitates your searching in two ways. First, if you have a partial citation or you have difficulty forming a query to find that document, you can use the Table of Contents feature to go directly to the section you are looking for.

Exhibit 3–4 Casemaker Logo.

Source: (**http://www.casemaker.us**). Used with the permission of Lawriter.

Table of Contents
like a book's table of contents, this feature lets you see what sections of the law are available and then easily access those sections.

Second, if you are unsure of what you want, or you know but cannot think of the right keywords, the Table of Contents feature lets you find the information by stepping through the law one section at a time.

Here is a summary of Casemaker's search features.

- **Boolean operators:** Casemaker does not technically use the traditional Boolean search operators. However, the *concept* of the Boolean search is there. For example:
  - To find all of the words (the equivalent to AND), you would simply enter the terms, each separated by a space. Thus, the AND equivalent is the default setting.
  - To find any of the words (the equivalent of OR), separate the words with a comma.
- **Proximity search:** You cannot do proximity searching in Casemaker.
- **Phrase search:** Casemaker permits phrase searching with single quotation marks. For example, you can search for the phrase *'unauthorized practice of law.'* As usual, the search ignores the stopword *of* (note that Casemaker refers to stopwords as noise words).
- **Stemming:** Casemaker uses the asterisk (*) for stemming and wildcard searching. You can put it before or after a word to expand the possible search terms. For example, if you search for the word *child**, Casemaker also looks for *children, childish,* and *childlike.*
- **Thesaurus Expansion:** Casemaker has a Thesaurus Expansion feature that yields results similar to stemming. When you insert the tilde (~) in front of a word, Casemaker will search for all related words. For example, similar to stemming, a search for the word *~child* also finds the words *children, childish,* and *childlike.* However, unlike stemming, the search would also yield documents with the words *kid, infant,* and *toddler.*

Casemaker's support materials and Help page offer more information on its search features.

Exercise 3-2

Review statements 1 through 5 in Exercise 3–1. How would the queries differ if you used your favorite smaller electronic database?

1. Whether non-profit organizations can sue when a donor fails to give a promised gift.
   a. query:
   b. source:
   c. hits:

2. Whether an environmental group can buy timber harvest rights when it has no intention of cutting wood.
    a. query:
    b. source:
    c. hits:

3. Whether a person who shares information with a bank for a loan has a right of privacy over personal information.
    a. query:
    b. source:
    c. hits:

4. Whether a nurse would lose her license if she took patient medication for personal use.
    a. query:
    b. source:
    c. hits:

5. Whether a college is liable for cleanup costs when an alum donates a piece of contaminated property.
    a. query:
    b. source:
    c. hits:

BEGINNING YOUR RESEARCH

In Chapter 2, we looked at Five Questions, a systematic way to begin a research project:

Question 1: What is the general legal topic?
Question 2: What type of law am I looking for?
Question 3: What secondary sources do I investigate?
Question 4: What source will I select to find the information?
Question 5: How do I formulate my query?

Let us use the Five Questions and your favorite paid legal database to explore the following scenario:

Eric Winiki rents a small, one-bedroom apartment for 12 months. When he moves in, he pays a $1000 refundable deposit. He has no written agreement with the landlord. Eric later decides to buy a condo and finds a perfect one not far away. When the closing date is determined, Eric writes a letter to give his landlord 30-days notice. Furious at Eric's short notice, the landlord refuses to return his deposit, despite the immaculate condition of the apartment. Eric wants to sue to get his deposit back. Can he prevail?

Question 1: What is the general legal topic?

Here, the general legal topic is *landlord tenant* law under the broader category of *real property*. Knowing these general topics helps you to focus your research.

Question 2: What type of law am I looking for?

Most states have a Landlord Tenant Act, which is *state statutory* law. In addition, there will probably be some cases on the subject. The cases are also likely to fall under state law.

Question 3: What secondary sources do I investigate?

If we keep focusing on state law, it might include some *state law review articles* that explain landlord-tenant law. Does your state have a *landlord tenant* or *real property practice book* for local attorneys? Such a resource may be available electronically via specialized databases. If not, do not be afraid to use any available printed resources. (The electronic researcher often forgets that books are still very useful.) Another resource might be a Web site of tenant rights advocates. Web sites are useful secondary sources in their own right. In doing a general Web search for tenants organizations or landlord tenant law in general, remember that it is state specific and whatever resources you find must relate directly to your state.

Question 4: What source will I select to find the information?

To answer this question, focus on a specific section of your paid legal database. Where exactly do you expect to find the answer? To find the actual Landlord Tenant Act, you should explore the statute section of your specific state. Some paid legal databases help you with this process. For example, Westlaw has a database wizard.

For secondary sources, stick with the state section, this time exploring the secondary source area. What relevant secondary sources are available in your state directory?

Question 5: How do I formulate my query?

To answer this question, you need to determine keywords. Sometimes crafting an issue statement can help you determine the keywords. Here, a good issue statement might be:

> *Whether a tenant can get his deposit back when he gave his landlord a 30-day notice and the parties had no other written agreement?*

Within this issue statement are some keywords for this topic: *tenant, deposit, notice.* Do you know why these were selected as keywords?

- **Tenant:** Although the legal topic is called landlord-tenant law, you rarely find a document that talks about tenants without also referring to or being relevant to landlords. So there is no need to use both words; just *tenant* (or *landlord*) works fine.

- **Deposit:** This term is the focus of our issue question—can Eric get his deposit back?

- **Notice:** This term is important because the landlord alleges insufficient notice is the reason for retaining the deposit.

Though you might be tempted to add *written agreement*, this phrase might eliminate some useful documents. Save it for a focus search if needed. Also, there is no need to include *30-day*, because it would again eliminate some useful documents.

Once you identify keywords, you are ready to put them together in a way that brings back the information you need. Formulating the query is the focus of the following Guided Exercises.

Guided Exercises

This Guided Exercise is designed to help you systematically explore how your favorite paid legal database works and how to find information there. Be patient and take notes. If you have a printed instruction manual for the paid legal database, write your notes right in the manual as you work through the exercise. That way, the notes are easily available to you later. If you have no manual, print the most relevant sections of the on-line Help manual, and use your printed pages as a handy reference.

Before you begin the Guided Exercise, take note of the following:

- Most paid legal databases do not let you query until after you select a specific database to search. Deciding on the appropriate database is part of the answer to Question 4 of the Five Questions.

terms and connectors used in Lexis to indicate Boolean search operators.

- Our lessons focus on Boolean or **terms and connectors** searching. Initially, Boolean searching can be more difficult than the natural language searching that both Lexis and Westlaw permit, but once you master it, terms and connectors searching yields much more specific results. When your employer bills for your time, your ability to effectively use Lexis and Westlaw becomes very important. Also, skills you learn doing Boolean searching on paid legal databases directly apply to your searching the Internet and other databases. For these reasons, focus on Boolean searching in this exercise and throughout the exercises in the text.

By far the easiest thing to do in paid legal databases is getting a document when you have an exact citation. However, it is in performing this simple task that some of the more frustrating mistakes occur. Here, we will try two different methods for finding a case and compare to see which is the most effective.

(continued)

1. **Go to your paid legal database.** Select a database for finding the landmark case *Miranda v Arizona*, 384 US 436 (1966). Remember to select the source most narrowly designed to meet your needs. For example, the U.S. Supreme Court is a federal body, so the database you select should include only federal, not state resources. Selecting a database narrowly suited to your needs limits the number of search results because you are searching fewer documents. Having fewer, more targeted results makes finding what you are looking for easier.

2. **Select a specific file in that database.** Remember to go narrow. Do not try to rush through the selection process. Read your options carefully. When you are more familiar with the options, you can select more quickly.

3. **Form a query.** The purpose of the query is to find the case *Miranda v Arizona*, 384 US 436 (1966). As you create your query, remember that all terms must have a connector. For example, if you want a case on the elements of battery, do not enter

   Elements battery

   Rather, you might enter

   Elements AND battery or

   Elements /s battery

   Note the connector between all terms. If you do not use a connector, the database automatically uses the default operator. Also note that you must place connectors between terms and you must not begin or end a query with a connector. What query did you enter for *Miranda v Arizona*? How many hits did you get? Evaluate your results—did you get what you wanted?[4]

4. **Find the same case by using the citation-specific search tool in your paid legal database.** In Lexis, this specific tool is called Lexsee,[5] in Westlaw it is Find. Loislaw's Advanced Search section permits a citation search. Now how many hits did you get?

When you search in the future for a single document with a citation, which method would you use and why?

Now let us try a more complicated activity—searching to find the answer to a scenario.

Your clients, Mr. and Mrs. Douglas, have a precocious eight-year-old son named Ricky. Last week, Ricky ventured into old Mr. Hanson's backyard (which closely resembles a junkyard), ignoring the no trespassing signs. Ricky had to climb a fence and bribe Mr. Hanson's dog with a bone to get to his goal—an old, rusty convertible. While playing in the old car, Ricky fell and broke his wrist. His parents want to sue Mr. Hanson for having such a dangerous yard in a neighborhood with several children. Mr. Hanson says he put up several barriers to entry and if the child ignored them and was injured, it was the child's fault. Do Mr. and Mrs. Douglas have a case?

Answer the Five Questions for this fact scenario.

Question 1: What is the general legal topic?
Question 2: What kind of law am I looking for?

Question 3: What secondary sources do I investigate?

Question 4: What source will I select to find this information? In other words, in what specific directory of my paid legal database will I look to find the information?

Question 5: How do I formulate my query? What keywords do I use? Refer to the following hints for help. Don't forget to use the hints that you learned in the previous section. See the end of the chapter for hints in answering this guided exercise.

- **Keyword Hint:** Remember that several words may be appropriate. Here, you may wish to use the word *injured* or *injury*. (Do not use the phrase *broken bones* or *broken wrist*—that is too specific.) You can use the OR connector or a wildcard operator like * or !. (The term *injur!* finds both *injured* and *injury*.)

- **Proximity Search Hint:** When searching for a fairly general term like *injury*, it is helpful to narrow the term by using other relevant keywords. However, you may also find that having your keywords close together is helpful. Using AND finds the keywords in the same document, but they might be completely unrelated, leading to lots of useless results. Suppose your keywords are *injury* and *child*. You might want to find *injury* and *child* in the same paragraph (/p) or in the same sentence (/s). One of this author's favorite connectors, however, is the number search (/n, where a number like 5 or 10 replaces the n). The number search works best with smaller numbers. If n is more than 10 or 15, you might as well use the sentence or paragraph proximity searches; both are very effective as well.

SUMMARY

As you learned while doing the exercises, there are more similarities than differences between the paid legal databases. Most use Boolean search operators as the basic method of retrieving documents from their vast databases. The comparison table at the end of the chapter shows just how similar the databases are.

In addition to looking at technical aspects of searching different databases, we looked at how to use a search strategy like the Five Questions to do research in the paid legal databases. If you continue to practice applying a search strategy when you research, you will find it becomes second nature and significantly speeds your research.

NOTES

1. Go to the Online Companion Web site that supports this text to find links to the tutorials.
2. *Discovering Westlaw*, 9th ed.
3. For Westlaw orientation links, see the Web site that supports this text.
4. When you do a typical query for a citation or party names, the database finds not only the document you requested, but every document that cites that document. For a case as famous as Miranda, that means a lot of documents. If available, use the hyperlinked reference to your case to find the actual text quickly.
5. Answers to the questions: What is your issue statement? *Whether Mr. Hanson is liable for injuries to a minor child who trespassed on his property?*
   What is the general topic of law involved? *Torts*
   What kind of law are you looking for? *Case law*
   Would it be state or federal? *State*
   In what source will you find the information? *Use the sources for your state cases.*
   What key words will you use? *trespass, minor, child, injury*

For additional resources, please go to http://www.paralegal.delmar.cengage.com

EXERCISES

Chapter Review Exercises

In Chapter 2, you prepared the Five Questions for the following fact scenarios. Now, do the actual research and answer the questions.

1. Greg and Erich entered into an agreement for Erich to buy a classic guitar from Greg for $950. They had no written agreement; the men just shook hands. Greg told Erich that the guitar would be ready in one week. When Erich arrived at the appointed time to get the guitar, Greg decided he did not want to sell. Erich wants to enforce the agreement. Can he?

2. Doug decided to rob the home of Sally. While in the house, Doug fell on a bicycle in the hall and sprained his ankle. Doug wants to sue Sally for negligence. Can he prevail?

3. After recovering from the sprained ankle, Doug decided to rob a jewelry store. Doug wore a black ski mask but was unarmed. When Doug entered the store, old Mr. Diamond was so horrified that he had a heart attack and died. Can Doug be charged for murder?

4. Javier and Raul buy an old beach house as joint tenants. For many years, the brothers enjoyed the house together. When Javier prepared his will, he left his part of the home to his son Joseph. Is his bequest valid?

5. Ken recently started having stomach problems. He thinks that during surgery five years ago, his doctor left a sponge in his tummy. He wonders if it is too late to sue the doctor for malpractice. Is it?

Exhibit 3–5 "Hey! There's that sponge . . . and my watch . . . are those my keys?!?"

Source: Illustration by Joe Mills. Reprinted with permission. All rights reserved.

Paid Legal Database Comparison Table

Database	Boolean (default in boldface)	Proximity Search	Phrase Search	Stemming	Wildcard
Westlaw	AND, **OR,** BUT NOT, /n	/s, +s /p, +p	"Quotation marks"	Automatic	* single letter ! at end of word
Lexis	AND, **OR,** NOT, /n, NOT /n	/s /p	"Quotation marks"	Automatic	* single letter ! at end of word
Loislaw	AND, **OR,** NOT, NEAR	NEAR#	"Quotation marks"	Automatic	? single letter * at end of word
Casemaker	space, comma	n/a	Single 'quotation mark'	~ tilde	* at beginning or end of word

Worksheet

New Database Worksheet

Use this worksheet to determine relevant search information when finding databases.

Database:

Boolean:

Proximity Search:

Phrase Search:

Stemming:

Wildcard:

Worksheet

Paid Legal Database Research Toolbox

Use this worksheet to comment on the Web sites featured in this chapter and to include information on your own favorites.

Web Site: Westlaw (**http://www.westlaw.com**)

Favorite Features:

Comments:

Web Site: Lexis (**http://www.lexis.com**)

Favorite Features:

Comments:

Web Site: Loislaw (**http://www.loislaw.com**)

Favorite Features:

Comments:

Web Site: Casemaker—available on the state bar Web sites of many states. For a current list of member states, visit (**http://www.casemaker.us**) and click on Contact.

Favorite Features:

Comments:

Internet Legal Research

CHAPTER

WELCOME TO THE INTERNET

The **Internet** is basically a collection of computers linked together. With the proper tools, you can connect your computer to other computers and get information from them. One part of the Internet is the **World Wide Web (WWW),** a collection of graphical interfaces that makes moving between pages and Web sites simple. The creation of the World Wide Web lowered the technical wall that separated techies from non-techies, making it easy for the most inexperienced person to enjoy the benefits of the Internet. The World Wide Web is also a great resource for the legal researcher, because it lets you do things that most people could not even imagine a decade ago. For example, from your home computer you can now do research that would have required you to spend time at a major law library. You can also access legal resources that you may not readily find in a law library—brief banks, forms, and so on. However, despite the convenience, the Internet is not a replacement for a physical law library or paid legal databases. For the most part, legal collections on the Internet are limited and are not as easily searchable as paid legal databases. For those reasons, the Internet is only one of many tools to use for legal research.

When doing any kind of research on the Internet, you need to know three things:

1. Where to look
2. How to look
3. How to determine the credibility of what you find

This chapter discusses each of those topics.

Internet
also known as the Net. A collection of linked computers that lets users review and exchange information. The Internet includes features like e-mail, telnet, bulletin boards, instant messaging, and the World Wide Web.

World Wide Web
also known as WWW or the Web. A collection of computers that enables users to access information through an appealing graphical interface. It lets Web sites have images, colors, and other interesting features, rather than just plain text.

WHERE TO LOOK FOR INFORMATION

The World Wide Web is a vast place and the best way to find information is to search for it using a **search engine**. The most popular search engine today is Google (**http://www.google.com**). Google is an incred-ibly powerful and innovative search engine that has made searching the Internet, once an arduous task, a simple activity that anyone can do. Indeed, with tools as powerful and easy to use as Google available, one may feel little need for instruction on how to search for information by using the Internet. However, by learning some of the behind the scenes details of how Google and other search engines work, your skill and flexibility in researching will greatly improve.

search engine
tool that lets you search through information on the Internet.

What Is a Search Engine?

A search engine is a tool used to search the Internet. It is similar to the search engines used in paid legal databases. Used generically, the term *search engine* includes all kinds of search tools. Most of the tools generally fit into one of three categories:

- search engines
- search directories
- specialty search tools

The next sections examine each of the tools.

Search Engines

A search engine searches the Web by using continuously running computer indexing programs known as crawlers or spiders. The spiders constantly scurry around the World Wide Web searching for new Web pages. They report their findings to the search engine. Search engine indexes are created automatically, and they contain the sites that the spiders find. So when you perform a search, you do not search the entire Web. Rather, you search the index created by the spiders. Many search engines advertise the size of their index. Google is reputed to have one of the largest indexes on the Internet. Size is not the only important indicator of a useful search engine. The other important point is how well the search engine can sift through its index to bring you back the most useful hits possible.

Using Google

The basic use of Google requires little instruction. If you visit its clean main page and type in a few search terms, you frequently find what you are looking for within the first 10 hits. The strategies that follow are to assist you when simple searching does not yield the results you want.

Google's Advanced Search

From Google's home page, click on the Advanced Search link to the right of the search box. The advanced search gives you access to many different search options. Here are just a few of them.

- **Boolean-like searching:** You can achieve Boolean-like precision by using Google's advanced search.
  - AND = all of the words
  - Phrase searching = this exact wording or phrase

- OR = one or more of these words
- NOT = but don't show pages that have any of these unwanted words
- **File format searching:** This option is helpful if you are looking for a sound file, a picture, a PowerPoint presentation, or any other kind of information where you know the type of file format. Use the dropdown menu to select the file type. You can also use Google Images (**http://images.google.com**) and Google Video (**http://video.google.com**).
- **Date:** Date searching is not as precise on the Internet as it is when you are using paid legal databases. However, you can limit your search to pages that have been recently updated. Google News (**http://news.google.com**) is also a good option for recent information.
- **Occurrences:** This is the equivalent of segment searching in Lexis or a field restricted search in Westlaw. Here, you can look for your terms in the Web page address (URL), the text of the page, the links, or the title. Searching the links is helpful so that you know what sites are linking to other sites.
- **Usage Rights:** This section of Google's advanced search helps you comply with copyright law. If you are searching for images, video, music, and so on on the Internet to use in legal presentations, you need to remember that most information on the Internet is protected by copyright. Thus, you generally need to get permission from the copyright holder to use the protected content. Google's Usage Rights feature enables you to do a search for open source content, where permission is more freely given for reuse.
- **Domain:** The Google search engine is so powerful that many Web sites have adopted it as their internal search tool. If you are trying to search a Web site that does not have very good search technology or, worse yet, no internal search at all, you can still use Google to search that Web site.

  To search a domain, put your search terms in the regular Find Results area at the top of the advanced search page. Then, specify that you want to search only a single site (rather than the entire Web index) by typing the specific Web address in the Domain box. Google will then search just that Web site for your search terms. You can also use this feature to omit certain sites from your search.

- **Topic-specific searching:** Google has many ways to organize its vast index to make it easier for you to find things. Its topic-specific searches are just one example of this. Near the bottom of the

Advanced Search page, you'll find the ever growing list of Google's topic-specific searches. Here are a few that you might find useful in your legal research.

- **Google News archive search (http://news.google.com/archivesearch):** The regular Google News search looks only for current news. Thus, if you are looking for something older, you will want to use the archive search feature.

- **Microsoft search (http://www.google.com/microsoft):** If you are wondering how to more effectively use your Microsoft Office products, you can easily find tutorials and other useful information by using this topic search, which returns only Web pages with information related to Microsoft.

- **U.S. Government search (http://www.google.com/ig/usgov):** This is probably the most useful topic-specific search for legal researchers. You can use this topic-specific search to access laws, agency guidance, explanatory documents, and more. This gives you simple access to any and all Web pages published by the U.S. government.

- **Google Product Search (http://www.google.com/products):** This is Google's shopping-specific search. In the legal office, a paralegal may be called on to use his or her skills to find legal software, office products, new technology, and more for the workplace. Google Product Search helps you to find the best prices with many useful price comparison features.

The Advanced Search features in Google are changing constantly, so regularly check out this page to see how Google is making yet another aspect of searching easier.

Pay to Play

When you enter a search query, you probably assume you are getting the most relevant information that the index has to offer. However, more and more Web site owners are willing to pay for the privilege of appearing high on your results list. If you run a search and get 58,000 hits, chances are you will look at only the first 10 to 20 sites listed. Web sites know this and are willing to pay to be among the top hits on your list. Look to see if your results are noted as "sponsored links." If so, someone has paid to appear at the top of your search results. Indeed, some search engines charge Web sites to even be included in their indexes. In Google, sponsored links appear on the left side of the screen and are not part of your search results. For other search engines, check the URL submission page to see if it charges Web sites to appear in the results list. You can generally find this information at the bottom of the search engine's home page as a link with a title like "Submit a Site."

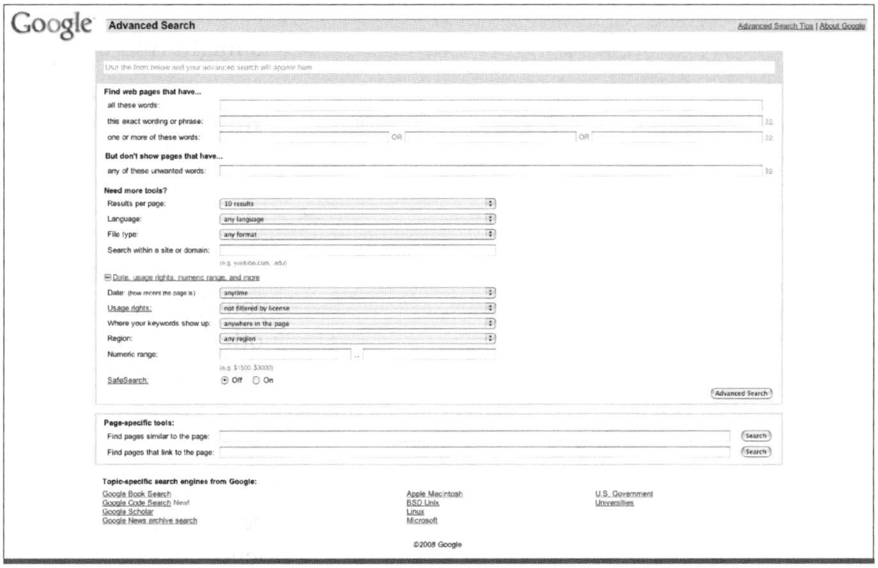

Exhibit 4–1 Google's advanced search page makes the Internet more accessible. From (**http://www.google.com**).

Source: Used with the permission of Google Inc. All rights reserved. Google is a trademark of Google Inc.

Beyond Google

With all of the power, speed, and ease of use associated with Google, you may wonder why you should even try other search engines. Although Google is an excellent tool, more great search engines are out there that are worthy of your consideration. For the most part, these search engines enable you to manipulate your results in ways that you can't with Google. Indeed, some of these search engines even use Google as their search engine and then use their search technology to manipulate the results. Here are a few search engines for you to try.

- **Ask.com (http://www.ask.com):** This Web site enables you to query a search engine by using natural language searching. This can be particularly helpful when you are having a difficult time determining what the best keywords would be for a search. By reviewing your results from a search on Ask.com, you can effectively adjust your query to get the results you want.

- **Clusty (http://www.clusty.com):** This Web site is a favorite choice when doing a very broad search that you are uncertain how to narrow. For example, imagine you are searching for information about torts. If you type *tort* into a search engine, you may get everything from negligence to desserts. Clusty clusters your search results into groups to make it easier to target your search. When you type *tort* into Clusty, you get results organized under the headings of tort reform, tort law, tort law firms, toxic torts, liability, wrongs, mass torts, personal injury and more. By clicking on one of the clusters, you see even more clusters and can effectively narrow your search.

- **All the Web (http://www.alltheweb.com):** This Web site is often recognized as the second best search engine on the web, after Google. Click on Advanced Search to access a host of special features, including the ability to do an actual Boolean search (many search tools have symbols instead of the regular Boolean search operators).

Search Directories

As mentioned earlier, the general term *search engine* encompasses many kinds of search technology. As noted, a search engine searches a large index of sites. The index is created automatically and the pages are not reviewed by people for their usefulness or accuracy. This is why you can do a search, get thousands of hits, and find most of them irrelevant or repetitive. Search directories offer a different option.

search directory
search tool that breaks sites into categories to facilitate browsing.

Search directories have indexes that are compiled automatically, but reviewed by people who sort the results into categories like Government, Entertainment, and Travel. This results in fewer, but frequently more relevant, hits. On the other hand, if you search for something rather obscure or something that does not fall into one of the categories, you may get no hits at all.

browsing
looking through ordered lists of information, generally arranged hierarchically, to find information you want. One might browse a table of contents or a subject area of directory.

Search directories also facilitate **browsing**. If you are not entirely sure what you are looking for, a directory makes it easy to start with a broad concept—like law—and work your way to a very specific concept—like sentencing.

Some top-ranked search directories include Yahoo! (**http://www.yahoo.com**) and Librarian's Index to the Internet (**http://www.lii.org**). Librarian's Index to the Internet is especially recommended, because a librarian has reviewed every site on the directory for usefulness, accuracy, and credibility.

Specialty Search Tools

Sometimes searching a large index of the World Wide Web for specific information is a bit too much. For specialty searches like legal or medical issues, you might wish someone would just find all law- or medicine-related sites and then let you search through them. Fortunately, **specialty search tools** grant your wish. One of the most popular specialty search engines for law is FindLaw (**http://www.findlaw.com**). Unlike most search tools, FindLaw has its own content in the form of laws, cases, forms, and other law-related content. It also searches the Internet for law-related content. The site is divided into sections for the

specialty search tools
search engines and directories dedicated to specific topics like law or medicine.

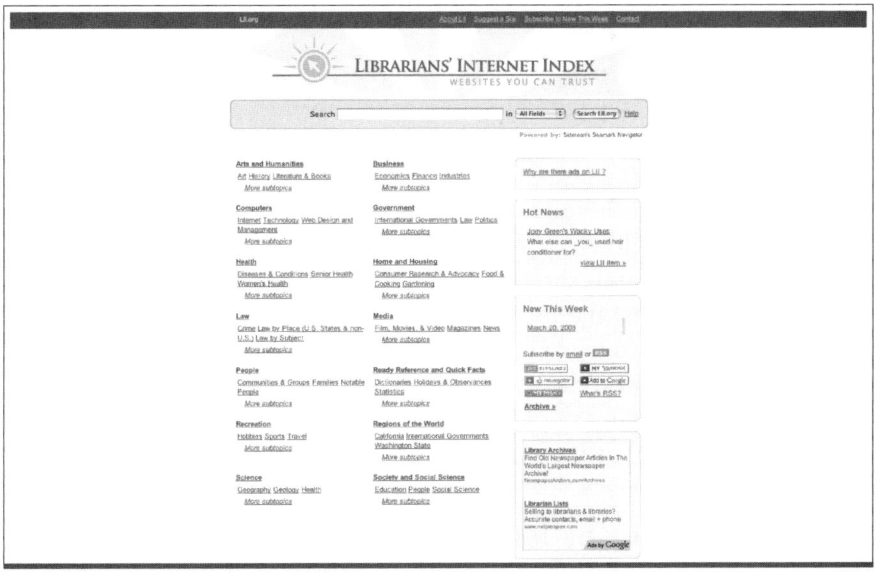

Exhibit 4–2 Every Web site in The Librarian's Index to the Internet
has been reviewed by a librarian for quality.

Source: From (**http://www.lii.org**)

public and for the legal community. Be sure to click on the For Legal Professionals tab at the top to access the site's most useful features, including the Reference Resources under the Practice Tools link (**http://
www.findlaw.com/15reference/**). Here you can easily access legal reference materials that are otherwise quite difficult to access.

The best way to find specialty search engines is to use a search engine
that looks for only other search engines. Try looking at the legal section
of Complete Planet (**http://www.completeplanet.com**) to see how
this works.

Exercise 4-1

Use at least three different search tools to search for explanations of the following legal concepts. Note how each tool varies.

	Search Engine	Search Directory	Specialty Search
Exhaustion of remedies			
Maritime law			
In loco parentis			
Negotiable instruments			

HOW TO LOOK FOR INFORMATION

When seeking information on the Internet, you generally move along a continuum from easy searching to more deliberate, difficult searching if you can't find what you want on the first effort. We will explore some of the steps along that continuum.

You should start your Internet search with a strategy, in the same way that you would start your paid legal database search. Because it is often easier to search the Internet, we have a simpler search strategy. Although searching the Internet can be easy, don't give into the temptation to abandon strategy altogether. If you have ever spent hours trying to find something on the Internet, you know that a good strategy is essential. The following steps will not only give you a good structure, they will save you a lot of time in the long run.

Step 1: Identify Key Terms and Search

For this first step, think about the best words to use for your search. This will be the basis for your searching and taking a moment or two to consider the most effective words is time well spent. Remember that search engines generally search for the words you are looking for to appear somewhere in the document. Let's say you are looking for a case about the unauthorized practice of law. It would not help to run a search with the key terms *case, unauthorized practice of law*. This is because many cases do not actually include the word *case* in them. You would be better off using something that actually does appear in a case, like *v.* (versus) if you would like your search to return cases. Many of the most frustrating searches are hampered by words that should be omitted from the search. Start simple and then narrow your search to get the best results.

Once you have selected the search terms that you would like to try, run your search using the search tool of your choice. Evaluate your results, adjusting your terms as needed. If, after a few minutes (no more than 5–10 minutes), you have not found what you are seeking, move on to step 2.

Step 2: Determine any Useful Narrowing and Search

If you did not find what you wanted in step 1, step 2 gives you the chance to be more precise in your searching. Sometimes you know at the outset that what you are seeking will require more focus and as such you might want to combine steps 1 and 2.

In this step, go to the Advanced Search page of your search tool. Optionally, you might want to try an alternate tool like Ask.com or Clusty to assist you in narrowing your search. Think about date restrictions, segment searching, and other advanced strategies that might help. Then run your search again. Try this step for another 5–10 minutes, exploring several options if needed. If your efforts are still unsuccessful, move on to step 3.

Step 3: Locate Subject Specific Web Sites and Search

If steps 1 and 2 did not get you the information you wanted, it may be useful to visit some subject-specific Web sites. Again, you may know as soon as you start strategizing that a specific Web site would be a useful place to start. If that is the case, combine steps 1 and 3.

It is in this step that you might try specialty search engines, agency Web sites, or law-specific resources. In the coming chapters, you will learn about several such resources that will be useful to you in your searching for statutes, regulations, cases, and secondary sources. Visit several Web sites and run your search on each (remember domain-specific searching in Google and All the Web if the Web site you visit does not have a good search tool). Once again, you want to spend only about 10 minutes on this step.

What Next?

If you try steps 1–3 and are still unable to find what you are looking for in 15–30 minutes, there might be several explanations for your lack of success. The two most common are that the information is not available for you to find or that the information does not exist or is not freely accessible on the Internet.

The Internet has a vast amount of information, but it is entirely possible that it does not have the thing you are looking for. For example, older cases can be difficult to find on the Internet. Some items may be only commercially available and require a paid subscription of some sort to access. Try running your search on a paid legal database to see if your query is more successful.

Your Search Query Needs Adjusting

Review your query to make sure it is effective for finding what you want. Omit any extra words that might be hampering your results. Try the simplest search you can think of, using just one or two terms and then adding terms to narrow as needed. Remember that search queries that are effective on one Web site may not be as effective on other Web sites. If you are doing a site-specific search, take a moment to review the site's Help section for additional information.

Exercise
4-2

Use the three step Internet search strategy to research the meaning of the following legal concepts. Use all three steps even if you find useful information more quickly. See if the information varies as you go deeper into the search. In the table's boxes, describe the types of results you found.

Step 1: identify the key terms and search
Step 2: determine any useful narrowing and search
Step 3: locate subject-specific Web sites and search

	Step 1 results	Step 2 results	Step 3 results
Practice of law			
Blue sky laws			
Whistleblower laws			

Guessing the URL

People often feel that searching is the only way to find information on the Web. Actually, if you basically know where you are going, performing a traditional search may not be the quickest way to get there. Do you take time to look up your best friend's phone number when you have it memorized? Probably not. By the same token, for many sites, if you know the company or organization name, you know its Web site address. Look at these examples:

- Delmar Cengage Learning (**http://www.delmar.com**)
- American Heart Association (**http://www.americanheart.org**)
- Environmental Protection Agency (**http://www.epa.gov**)

The tricky thing to remember is the kind of place you are trying to access. Is it a company or business that sells things? If so, chances are its URL has the *.com* suffix. Is it a government agency? Expect the *.gov* suffix. How about a club, group, or other non-profit organization? Expect to see the *.org* suffix at the end of its name. Finally, if you are looking for a college, university, grade school, or other educational institution, tack *.edu* on the end.

Here are some additional hints to assist you in guessing and remembering Web addresses.

- If the name is long, try using an abbreviation, for example, NYU for New York University (**http://www.nyu.edu**).
- International organizations often add *America*, *USA*, or *US* to their Web site names, for example, Toyota USA (**http://www.**

toyotaUSA.com) or the United States Supreme Court (**http://www.supremecourtus.gov**).

- Remember that a Web site address contains no spaces. For example, the Sierra Club is (**http://www.sierraclub.org***)*.

These strategies are helpful not only in guessing a Web address, they also help you remember the address so that you don't have to search for it next time. This is especially handy when you are working at a computer where you do not have your bookmarks available.

Bookmarks on the Move

You probably find yourself using many different computers during any given week. You may have one at home, one at work, and a laptop. You may use computers in a lab at school or in a library. With all of this moving around, it is great to have bookmarks or favorites that move with you. Here are some options.

Del.icio.us (http://del.icio.us/): With this site, you can save all of your bookmarks and see what others are bookmarking as well. Because your bookmarks are accessed through the Internet, you could access them wherever you get online. Try visiting Del.icio.us and doing a search for *"legal research"* to see what websites are the most popular. To find other sites like Del.icio.us, try doing a web search for *"social bookmarking."*

Google Toolbar (http://toolbar.google.com): Google's handy toolbar will give you access to your favorites wherever a Google toolbar is installed. You can do the same thing with Yahoo! Bookmarks (**http://bookmarks.yahoo.com**)

Powermarks (http://www.kaylon.com/power.html): If you have a lot of bookmarks (this author has around 2000), trying to organize them in a Favorites list can be impractical. Fortunately, tools like Powermarks automatically create searchable keywords of your bookmarks. So when you need a bookmark, you don't need to scroll through a long list. You can just do a quick keyword search and it will pop up. Powermarks can be installed on every computer you use and you can synchronize them using the Internet. Thus, you have your bookmarks with you all of the time.

YOUR INTERNET TOOLBOX

The Internet is full of lists of links telling you the *best* places to find information. But what determines whether a site is the *best*? Different people would answer the question differently. For the businessperson, the best site might be the one that gets the most hits. For the Web developer, it might be the site with the best design. For you, as a legal researcher, the answer will depend on what you are looking for. However, the researcher should consider a few basic criteria that fall under two categories: information and technology.

A heightened awareness of information and technology issues can help you evaluate which sites are better than others. As an effective legal researcher, it is important that your research information come from only the most credible and reliable sources, preferably those that are well organized and maintained. Remember, your client depends on it.

When researching, your collection of favorite sites will be what facilitates your effective legal research. You should never be completely satisfied with your list; make a point to read legal Weblogs, newsletters, and journals to find new and better sites to add to your list. Also, don't forget to discard sites that no longer serve your needs. Throughout the coming chapters, you will build a site collection that will be the foundation of your effective Internet researching for years to come.

HOW TO DETERMINE THE CREDIBILITY AND USEFULNESS OF WHAT YOU FIND

The Internet is a mountain of information. Your first challenge is to find what you are looking for. Your second challenge is to determine whether what you found is both credible and useful. Anyone can create a Web site and post on it any information they choose. Not all the information is true or credible. This is true of any media. However, on the Internet and on the sites you visit, you must be especially vigilant in determining the validity of information. Even if the information is true, it may not be very useful. Evaluating the usefulness also helps you to delve deeper into the credibility of the site.

Credibility of Information

When thinking about credibility, ask yourself whether the information on the Web site is true. Because anyone can post anything on the Internet, you cannot get into the habit of taking what you see at face value. You must think critically about the information. Fortunately, making an initial determination of a site's credibility is fairly easy. You can do it by asking two key questions: What is the purpose of this site? How current is the information?

What is the Purpose of this Site?

When looking for credible information on the Internet, being aware of why the information is there is essential. Is it there to educate? Are the site sponsors trying to sell you something? Are they trying to persuade you to take a certain viewpoint? One way to determine a site's purpose is to think about who placed the site on the Internet. Generally, Web site sponsors belong to one of four groups: educational or governmental organizations, businesses, non-profit organizations, and individuals.

Educational Institutions or Government Organizations

These sites are usually a safe bet for credible information, but you should still be alert. Generally, their purpose is to educate the visitor. However, you should be cautious about individual student Web sites. With a *.edu* extension, student Web sites look like school-sponsored sites. However, most schools that let students create personal Web sites are not involved in those sites' content. Consider them in the same manner as you consider individuals' sites.

Businesses

Generally, these sites have a financial motive for providing information. Businesses want to educate you or tempt you to buy their products. That does not mean that the information is not credible, but it does mean that you should look at the information a little more critically. Check the validity of the information by seeing if you can find similar information on other sites.

Exhibit 4–3 University of Washington's Gallagher Law Library. Information provided by educational institutions is generally very useful.

Source: From (**http://lib.law.washington.edu**)

Law Firm Web Sites

More and more law firms are on the Internet and providing useful information. Do not be less vigilant because the information comes from a lawyer. Law firms are businesses too.

Non-Profit Organizations
These organizations generally have biases that you should be aware of. Indeed, all information is biased in some manner, so thinking critically about information that you encounter helps to heighten your awareness of information that is biased. However, just because an organization presents information for a biased reason does not mean that the information is not useful. It may mean, however, that the site does not present you with both sides of an issue.

Individuals
If information seems to come from an individual, examine the person's credentials and make sure the person has the background to present information authoritatively. If no credential information is available, treat the information even more cautiously.

How Current is the Information?

The second question you should ask when determining the credibility of information is whether the information is up to date. Law is in a constant state of flux, changing with every court decision and every legislative session. That means that the information may have been perfectly true when it was posted, but is no longer true now. The time-sensitive nature of legal information makes it essential that you consider the timeliness of your information when on the Internet. This is not a concern on paid legal databases because the current status of the databases is one of the things you are paying for.

Not all information is time sensitive, however. For example, a legal decision made in 1984 is not going to change. However, the impact of that case on the law and the current status of the law might change, making that information time sensitive. Thus, you have to make the determination of whether information is time sensitive. If you need time sensitive information, check to see when the Web site was last updated. Some sites are placed on the Web and not updated for months or even years. The Last Updated date is often at the bottom of a page in small print. If that information is not available, you should be especially cautious with time sensitive information. Check other Web sites or go to your paid legal database to confirm the information.

Usefulness of Information

Even if the information is true, it may not be very useful. Here are some tips for evaluating the usefulness of information. You want to include only the most useful Web sites in your research toolbox.

- Is the information on the site trustworthy? Did the site pass the credibility questions with flying colors? If not, you should probably not include it in your legal research favorites—although you may enjoy the site for other purposes.

- Is the information easy to find? It does not matter if a Web site has great information if you have to spend all afternoon trying to find it. Does the site have an internal search engine? A site map?

- Is the information complete? Does the site seem to have all the information you want on a given subject, or does the site link you to other sites for related information? If you do have to go to other sites for information, remember to review the linked site's credibility as well. One credible site that links to another site does not guarantee the credibility of the second site.

- Is the freely available information substantive? Often Web sites just skim the surface of legal topics. The best sites have in-depth information that tells you more than you already know. They also have free substantive information. Some sites hint at their content and then make you pay to see the full document. In general, the Web offers so much free information that you generally should not have to pay. When information is hard to find or its credibility is hard to determine, then you might want to go to Westlaw, Lexis, or another paid legal database. Much information for sale on the Web is available as part of the vast Westlaw and Lexis databases.

- Is the site well maintained? Well maintained sites have links that go to their intended places and time sensitive information that is kept up to date. If the site is frequently unavailable or slow, that may indicate inadequate maintenance.

**Exercise
4-3**

Use this exercise to begin compiling your own list of favorite sites for your research toolbox. Use the set of site evaluation worksheets at the end of the chapter to complete this exercise. These worksheets are also available in a printed format in the Online Companion to this text.

1. Use the site evaluation worksheet to determine why these three legal research sites are so popular.

   • Hieros Gamos (**http://www.hg.org**)

   • Cornell Law School (**http://www.law.cornell.edu**)

   • Law.com (**http://www.law.com**)

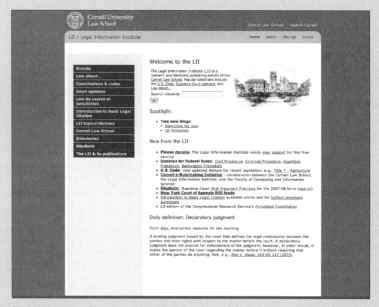

Exhibit 4–4 Cornell Law School's Legal Information Institute.

Source: From (**http://www.law.cornell.edu**). Used with the permission of the Legal Information Institute, Cornell Law School.

2. Use skills that you learned in this chapter to find and evaluate three more legal research sites. Try to focus on sites with legal information specific to your state (see the State Law Library box for ideas). Be sure to pick sites that are not mentioned in this text.

Few people know more about legal research than state law librarians. The Web site of your state law library is an excellent source of information about on-line legal research in your state. Just search the name of your state and *"state law library"* in your favorite search engine. For a great example, check out the Wisconsin State Law Library at (**http://wsll. state.wi.us/**). The law school libraries in your state are also wonderful places to look for state-related materials.

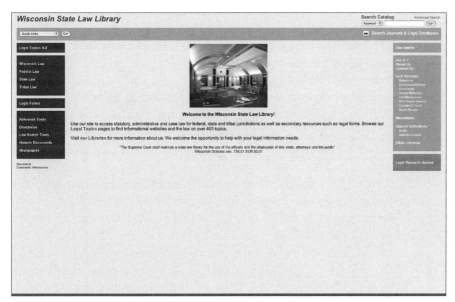

Exhibit 4–5 Wisconsin State Law Library. State law library web sites give you great access to state resources on the Internet.

Source: Used with permission of the Wisconsin State Law Library. From (**http://wsll.state.wi.us**)

FREE VERSUS PAID

This chapter discussed the skills needed to do legal research on the Internet. It also looked at the strengths and weaknesses of information the Internet provides. However, the chapter has not yet covered when to use the Internet instead of a paid legal database. You must make this determination on a case-by-case basis. Frequently, though, the Internet will be just one part of your fuller research strategy. The Internet can be a quick and easy way to begin your research and you can delve deeper using paid legal databases. As you become more familiar with the resources available, you will figure out which tools you like using to find different types of information. Many exercises in this text encourage you to try the same exercise using several different sources so that you can get a feel for which works better for each different task. Avoid taking the lazy way and always starting at the same point without thinking about the kind of information you are looking for. Just a few minutes of strategizing may save you a significant amount of research frustration.

SUMMARY

The World Wide Web provides the legal researcher with a vast array of resources for effective legal research. Your task as a legal researcher is finding the best and most credible information. This chapter looked at the various search tools and explored their features so that you can use them in the most effective way possible.

The chapter also presented a strategy for searching on the Internet. After finding the information, evaluating its credibility is important. Simply being aware of credibility issues helps, but asking a couple of questions about credibility and usefulness can ensure that your research efforts are not based on bad information.

Searching for information on the Web can be really easy or really challenging. As a skilled researcher, you should have a list of sites that facilitate finding information quickly so that you can move more of your searches into the really easy category. This chapter discussed how to create such a list and how to make sure your choices are among the best.

This chapter is just an introduction to doing legal research on the Internet. Throughout the chapters in the second part of this text, you will practice the skills you learned in this chapter so that, in the end, you will be an effective electronic legal researcher, regardless of the information sources.

EXERCISES

Chapter Review Exercises

Answer the following questions by using Internet resources. Use the three step Internet strategy or the Five Questions to assist your research.

1. Gabriella recently bought a piece of property with an easement across one corner, permitting public access to a stream. The stream has been dry for years, and it appears to Gabriella that no one has used the easement for a long time. Now, Gabriella wants to put a garden room on a portion of the easement. What steps does she need to take to do this?

2. Your attorney is drafting a lease for a corporate client. She wants to include a clause that would require the parties to go to mediation if a dispute arises under the contract. Can you suggest some language?

3. Lucy and several other volunteers were on a charter flight to a small Latin American nation where they were to work as missionaries. There was great political unrest in the country, and all the volunteers were very nervous. The in-flight movie was about a group of missionaries who were brutally killed during political unrest. The movie upset Lucy very much, causing her to suffer from insomnia for weeks, eventually abandon her mission, and return home only a few weeks after arriving. Lucy wants to sue the airline for intentional infliction of emotional distress. Are the elements for that tort met in this situation?

4. Your attorney is interested in comparing the language of the Uniform Commercial Code on the Statute of Frauds to the Statute of Frauds language adopted by your state. Can you find the two sections?

5. You volunteer with a non-profit organization that delivers legal services to the poor. The organization decides to collect some Web resources to help their pro se clients. Can you suggest three or four high quality Web sites? Be sure to review the sites carefully for useful content. You may find the Web site evaluation worksheet helpful for answering this question.

Worksheet

Web Site Evaluation Worksheet

Name of Site _____

Site Address _____

For the following information, use a scale of 0–2 for a high score of 14.

    0 = bad
    1 = good
    2 = very good

Is the information credible? Score _____

Comments:

_____

Is the information easy to find? Score _____

Comments:

_____

Is the information complete? Score _____

Comments:

_____

Is the information substantive? Score _____

Comments:

_____

Is the site well maintained? Score _____

Comments:

Worksheet

Internet Research Toolbox

Use this worksheet to comment on the Web sites featured in this chapter and to include information on your favorites.

Web Site: Google (http://www.google.com)

Favorite Features:

Comments:

Web Site: Ask.com (**http://www.ask.com**)

Favorite Features:

Comments:

Web Site: Clusty (**http://www.clusty.com**)

Favorite Features:

Comments:

Web Site: All The Web (**http://www.alltheweb.com**)

Favorite Features:

Comments:

Web Site: Yahoo! (**http://www.yahoo.com**)

Favorite Features:

Comments:

Web Site: Librarian's Index to the Internet (**http://www.lii.org**)

Favorite Features:

Comments:

Web Site: FindLaw (**http://www.findlaw.com**)

Favorite Features:

Comments:

Web Site: Wisconsin State Law Library (**http://wsll.state.wi.us/**)

Favorite Features:

Comments:

What to Search for

II

Finding and Understanding Statutes

CHAPTER 5

CHAPTER OBJECTIVES

- **Review of statutory law:** What are statutes? How do they differ from regulations and other kinds of law?
- **Statute search strategies:** Depending on the information you have to start with, there are different strategies for finding a statute when you have a citation, a statute name, or a topic.
- **Statutory interpretation:** After finding the statutes, you often need to interpret them to complete your research. In this chapter, you learn the basic rules of statutory interpretation.

ON THE WEB

- http://www.paralegal.delmar.cengage.com
- Annotated links leading you to:
  - How a bill becomes a law
  - The federal legal system
  - How to research legislative history
- Exercises for additional help

REVIEW OF STATUTORY LAW

statute
also known as an act or code. A law created by the legislative branch of government.

act
see statute.

Statutes, or **acts**, are broad pronouncements of law created by legislative bodies at the federal or state level. When searching for statutes, you must be aware of several basic issues of legal research.

First, you must clearly understand the difference between state and federal law. Sometimes state and federal laws have similar names and regulate in similar ways. For example, Pennsylvania has the *Banking Code of 1965*, 7 P.S. §101, *et seq*. To confuse you, the federal government has the *Banking Act of 1933*, 12 USC 227. So, you can see why knowing whether you are looking for state or federal law is important. If you look in the federal code for a state law, you will be very frustrated.

Next, you need to make sure that what you want is a statute and not a regulation or case law. Determining the difference is often hard, but keep the following in mind:

- Statutes are generally broad, whereas regulations are more detailed, filling in the specifics of the broad statutory pronouncements. (For more information on regulations, see Chapter 7.)
- Statutes authorize regulations.
- Congress and your state legislature create statutes. Administrative agencies create regulations.
- Statutes often contain the word *Act* (as in the Clean Air Act) or *Code* (as in the Tax Code).

Once you are certain you are looking for a statute, keep in mind that most statutes have several sections. When you search documents in an electronic format, each section registers as a hit. So, if you look for the Clean Air Act, for example, you get dozens of hits, indicating each separate section of the act. If the Clean Air Act has 50 sections, you get at least 50 hits, all of which are correct. If you do a search based on the act's title, you can narrow your search by using the name of the act, plus keywords specific to what you are looking for in the act. For example:

"Clean Air Act" AND permit NEAR emission

Another important thing to remember when researching statutes is that an administrative agency enforces most statutes. For example, the Environmental Protection Agency enforces the Clean Air Act. You can often guess which agency might enforce a statute from the subject matter. Knowing the enforcing agency is helpful because it might give you more options for doing your research. For example, many agencies use their Web sites to post the full text of laws they enforce, along with helpful explanatory materials in plain English. The federal Web site FirstGov (**http://www.firstgov.gov**) has links to all federal agencies and many state agencies as well.

STATUTE SEARCH STRATEGIES

Finding statutory law electronically can be challenging—especially if you are used to researching "by the book." Books let you browse through a statute, flip pages, and generally stumble around until you find what you are looking for. Because statutes tend to be long and contain several parts, stumbling around can be a very useful way to go. Unfortunately, electronic resources are not as stumble friendly. To succeed in searching most electronic resources for a statute, you really need to know what you are looking for.

You can sometimes mimic flipping pages by browsing through an electronic table of contents. Browsing is particularly helpful if you know the name of the law you are looking for or if you would know it when you see it. Browsing also gives you the advantage of a book—you can look through a table of contents to see what might be there. When you find what you need or get better keywords, you can do a more specific search if needed. As you will learn later in the chapter, not all electronic resources allow for browsing, so you want to become familiar with those that offer this useful feature.

When looking for a statute, you generally have at least one of these pieces of information

- citation
- statute name
- topic

The next section explores how to find a statute by using those pieces of information with paid legal databases and on the Internet.

Research Strategies

BEFORE YOU BEGIN YOUR STATUTE SEARCH, ASK THESE QUESTIONS:

- Do I really want a statute?
- Do I want a state or a federal statute?
- Which agency might enforce the statute?

citation

abbreviated method of referring to a source of information. Found in both legal and non-legal documents, citations follow a specific format. In legal writing, the main resource for legal citation format is the *Bluebook*.

code

see statute.

Finding Statutes with Citations

Finding a statute with a **citation** is the best of all possible research positions. From the citation, you can easily tell whether you are searching for state or federal law. Federal statutes are located in the United States Code (USC). Locations of state citations vary, but their titles often include the word *code*, *statute*, or *laws*. For example, Oklahoma has the Oklahoma Statutes (OS), and West Virginia has the West Virginia Code (WVC).

Westlaw Searching

Westlaw's Find tool makes pulling up a document easy when you know the citation. Simply type your citation in the Find this Document by Citation box. When using Westlaw, keep in mind that you do not have to use periods or other proper citation indicators to access the requested document. For example, you could shorten 33 U.S.C. §151 to *33 usc 151* and still locate the document.

Instructions: To use Find this Document by Citation to find a statute by citation:

1. Go to the Find this Document by Citation search box on the main page.
2. Enter your citation in the search box and click on the Go button.
3. If you have trouble pulling up your desired document, check Help to ensure you entered your citation correctly.

Make sure that you enter your citation in the right place. Frequently, students enter a citation in the regular Westlaw search box. Though this does find your statute, it also finds cross-references to it—dozens of generally frustrating hits. If cross-references are what you want, this is a great way to get them. But if you are just searching for a single statute section, using Find is a good approach.

Lexis Searching

Lexis has a feature called Get a Document that lets you quickly and easily pull up a statute by using a citation. When using Get a Document, keep in mind that you do not have to use periods or other proper citation indicators. For example, you could shorten *33 U.S.C. §151* to *33 usc 151* and get the same results.

Frequently, students do not enter their citations in the proper place. They enter a citation in the regular Lexis search box. They find the statute that they are looking for, but they also find dozens of cross-references. This is a great method for finding cross-references, but an inefficient way to search for a single statute section. Get a Document is preferred for more targeted searching.

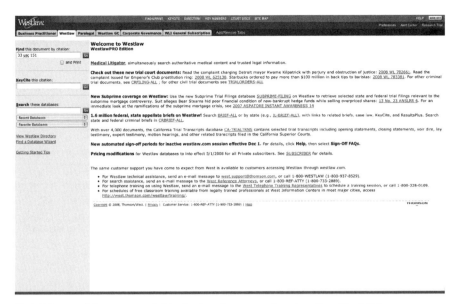

Exhibit 5–1 You can quickly find a document using the Find this Document by Citation search box.

Source: From the Westlaw Web site, (**http://www.westlaw.com**). Used with the permission of West Group.

Instructions: To use Get a Document to find a statute by citation, do the following:

1. Click on the Get a Document tab at the top of the screen.
2. You have three choices on the left: Citation, Party Name, and Docket Number. Choose Citation.
3. Enter your citation in the search box and click on the Get button.
4. If you have trouble pulling up your desired document, check the Citation Formats link next to the Citation search box to ensure you entered your citation correctly.

Loislaw Searching

In Loislaw, you can easily get a statute by using the citation if you select the proper database and enter the citation in the regular search box. Be careful to check Help for the correct citation format: Loislaw is not as forgiving as Westlaw and Lexis.

Instructions: To find a statute by using a citation in Loislaw, follow these steps:

1. Click on the Statutes and Acts database.
2. Select the jurisdiction (specific state or federal) that you want to search. You can select multiple jurisdictions if you are unsure of the correct one. Click on Continue at the bottom of the page.

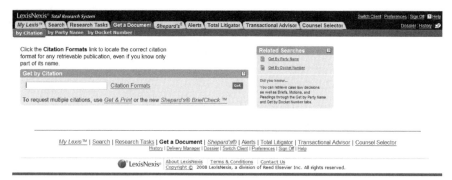

Exhibit 5–2 Lexis makes it easy to get documents by citation.

Source: From the Lexis-Nexis Web site, (**http://www.lexis.com**). Copyright 2006 LexisNexis, a division of Reed Elsevier Inc. All Rights Reserved. LexisNexis and the Knowledge Burst logo are registered trademarks of Reed Elsevier Properties Inc. and are used with the permission of LexisNexis.

3. Enter your citation in the search box.
4. If you have trouble pulling up your desired document, check the Help section to ensure that you used the correct citation format.

Casemaker Searching

In Casemaker, you can do a citation search by using the Advanced Search box. Be careful to check Help for the correct citation format: Casemaker is not as forgiving as Westlaw and Lexis.

Instructions: To find a statute by using a citation in Casemaker, follow these steps:

1. In Casemaker, access your state library.
2. Choose your state's statutes library.
3. When you get the search box, click on the Advanced Search tab.
4. Enter your citation in the Citation search box. Check to confirm that any options for the type of citation you are entering have been selected.
5. If you have trouble pulling up your desired document, check the Help section to ensure that you used the correct citation format.

Internet Searching

Several law-related search tools let you search the limited United States Code database with a citation. One such site is FindLaw (**http://www.findlaw.com**).[1] This search tool is not as exact as those of paid legal databases, but it works well. Your search is likely to yield many results, because it may bring up cross-references. Try searching your citation as a phrase to get better results.

Browsing is also available on many Internet sites. Remember, statutes often have several sections. You may have a statute reference that notes only the first section. For example, 23 USC 453, *et sec. Et seq* means *and*

et seq

Latin phrase meaning *and the following sections.* Statutory citations often use this phrase where the first section of the statute is cited and the rest are included.

all the following sections. When this is the case, your citation takes you to the beginning of the statute. Unfortunately, what you need may be somewhere within the statute. If so, try browsing through the table of contents to find relevant information.

Browsing in a paid legal database can be complicated, but some Web sites make it fairly straightforward. Try the Legal Information Institute Web page at Cornell Law School (**http://www.law.cornell.edu**).[2] The U.S. Code has an easy to use title and section search as well as the table of contents for browsing or searching. The handy Search link next to each Title section enables you to search just that section of the code, which will speed up your search and limit your results.

Instructions: To find a document by using a citation when you're in the Legal Information Institute, follow these steps:

- From the Legal Information Institute Web site (**http://www.law. cornell.edu**), click on Constitutions and Codes.
- Scroll down just a bit to the section titled Find US Code Materials by Title and Section.
- Enter the title and section in the appropriate boxes and click on Go to Title and Section to retrieve your document.
- Use the How Current is This? link just below the title to get updated information on the statute.

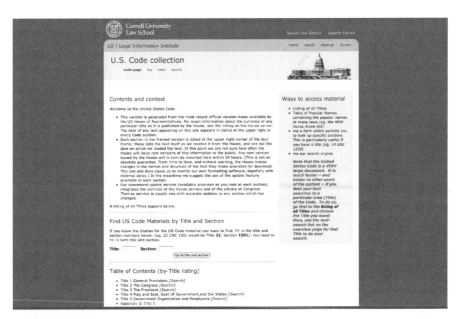

Exhibit 5–3 You can search the United States Code on the Legal Information.

Source: Institute website from Cornell Law School. From (**http://www.law.cornell.edu**). Used with permission of the Legal Information Institute, Cornell Law School.

You often have more than one resource for finding the information you need. The skilled researcher knows the most efficient way to find the best information. Use this exercise to determine the most efficient way to find a statute by using a citation.

1. Look up the following citations by using both the Internet and a paid legal database.
2. In the space provided and using your personal research standards, indicate the pros and cons of each search method.

	Paid Legal Database		Internet	
Citation	**Pros**	**Cons**	**Pros**	**Cons**
42 USC 1201				
16 USC 1151				
21 USC 1054				
42 USC 14301				
28 USC 134				
4 USC 8				

Finding Statutes with a Title

When you only have a statute title, you generally use more traditional, Boolean-style searching. Try using phrase searching for better results.

Westlaw Searching

field restricted search
in Westlaw, a search of specific portions of a document like the title, author, or parties.

If you know the title of the statute, you can do what is known as a **field restricted search**.

Instructions: To find a statute by title in Westlaw, follow these steps:

1. Select your database. You can enter the code for the database directly or you can use the Find a Database Wizard.
2. Once you have selected your database, you will have a search box available. On the lower part of the search box is a Fields dropdown menu. Choose Preliminary.
3. Remember: If your query has more than one word, be sure to include your connectors.

To narrow your search, you can use other relevant keywords as part of your title search. Depending on the database you choose, you get not only the statute but also supporting and referring documents.

For example, if you are looking for the Endangered Species Act and your focus is the meaning of the word *habitat*, you might try the query:

"Endangered Species Act" AND habitat

Lexis Searching

Lexis offers two ways to do a title search. Using the first method, **segment searching**, you search individual segments of a document. For example, you can search the title, the citation, the date, and so on. If you know the title, you search the Heading segment, because you know the title, which appears in the Heading of the statute. Even when you use segment searching, you can use additional keywords, connecting them with the usual Boolean operators.

segment searching
in Lexis, a search of specific portions of a document, such as the title, author, or parties.

Instructions: To find a statute by using the title, follow these steps:

1. From the main page of Lexis, select your desired jurisdiction by clicking on its name (e.g., "United States Code Service—Titles 1 through 50").
2. Make sure the search option is Terms and Connectors.
3. Below the search box, you will see options to search the full text of source documents or to search table of contents (TOC) only. Choose Full-text source of documents.
4. The search box will change slightly. In the middle of the search box, you will see Restrict using Mandatory Terms and below that, you will see a dropdown menu where you can select a segment.
5. Choose Heading from the dropdown menu and click on Add.
6. Click on Search to pull up your document.

Additionally, you can do a search of the Popular Names Table. Or you can also do a general search and use quotation marks around the statute name (e.g., "Endangered Species Act"). This searches for the title of the act anywhere within the text of the documents.

Do not forget to select the proper source. Remember, you cannot find what you are looking for if you look in the wrong source. To narrow your search, you can use other relevant keywords. Depending on the source you choose, you get not only the statute but also supporting and referring documents. For example, if you are looking for the Endangered Species Act and your focus is the meaning of the word *habitat*, you might try this query:

"Endangered Species Act" AND habitat

Loislaw Searching

In Loislaw, you can search for a statute by name by selecting the proper database and entering the statute name in the Title space.

Instructions: To find a statute by using a statute name in Loislaw, follow these steps:

1. Click on the Statutes and Acts database.
2. Select the jurisdiction (state or federal) that you want to search. You can select multiple jurisdictions if you are unsure of the correct one.
3. Enter your statute name in the search box.
4. If you have trouble pulling up your desired document, check the Help section to ensure that you used the correct citation format.

Casemaker Searching

In Casemaker, you can use the advanced search feature to search directly for statutes by citation.

Instructions: To use a citation to find a statute in Casemaker, follow these steps:

1. In Casemaker, access your state library.
2. Choose your state's statutes library.
3. When you get the search box, click on the Advanced Search tab.
4. Enter your statute name in the Title search box.

Internet Searching

If you have the name of the act and you are doing an Internet search, you can just enter the title in your favorite search tool, like Google (**http://www.google.com**) or FindLaw (**http://www.findlaw.com**). It is likely that the statute that you are seeking will appear in one of the first search results.

Additionally, you may want to go directly to the source. Many agencies at the federal level post their statutes on their Web sites. The advantage of using an agency Web site is that these sites generally have a great deal of explanatory information in addition to the statute. This is helpful when you are researching a statute that you are not very familiar with and you want to try some strategizing before you search. Because agencies administer most federal acts, going to the agency's Web site can be the easiest way to find the act you want. You might also discover explanatory documents in plain English. Use the Web site's internal search tool (if it has one) and try placing quotation marks around the act's title to facilitate your search. Even if the agency's Web site does not have the actual text of the statute you want, it might have discussions about the act that contain useful citations to can help you do a more direct search. Use FirstGov (**http://www.firstgov.gov**) to find links to all federal and many state agencies.

Exhibit 5–4 FirstGov.gov. FirstGov is a portal to all federal and local government information.

Exercise 5-2

Find the following statutes at either the state or the federal levels. Your state act's name might differ slightly—ask your instructor for clarification.

1. Use both a paid legal database and the Internet for your search.
2. Note the proper starting citation when you find the act.
3. Note the pros and cons of each method of searching.

	Paid Legal Database		Internet	
Citation	*Pros*	*Cons*	*Pros*	*Cons*
Clean Water Act:				
Public Records Act:				
Highways or Transportation Code:				
Education Code:				

Exercise 5-3

To complete this exercise, answer the following questions:

1. Are your state's statutes available on the Internet? Where?
2. Are the statutes searchable? Browsable? Both?
3. How would you use a paid legal database to access your state's statutory materials?
4. Which statutory materials are located there?

Finding Statutes by Using a Topic

Finding a statute when you have only a topic generally requires traditional Boolean-style searching. So choosing good keywords and searching the appropriate databases are important. Before you start your search, clearly identify whether your statute is a state or a federal law. Remember that your search can only succeed when you do it in the right place.

Guided Exercise: Westlaw or Lexis Searching

Once you select the appropriate database, you use your basic Westlaw or Lexis, skills to find the statute itself.[3] Let us look at an example.

Our client, Maryanne Gato, has been a connoisseur of fine wines for many years. Recently, she decided to open her own winery. She believes that wine labels are subject to federal regulation, and she wants your firm to find the specifics of those regulations. Your job is to find the relevant statute.

Exhibit 5–5 E.B. Foote wine label.

Source: Courtesy of E.B. Foote Winery.

1.   **Determine whether the law is a state or a federal law.** You have been told that the law is federal.

2.   **Identify appropriate databases.** Here, simply choosing the United States Code (USC) is your best bet because you want to start with the narrowest database.

3.   **Brainstorm to identify keywords.** For this exercise, you might choose the keywords *wine* and *label*. In forming your query, remember that the word *labels* may appear in several forms—*labels, labeling,* and so on. So here is your query:

     wine and label!

     This query yields more than 100 documents. Narrow the search by using Westlaw's Locate or Lexis' Focus feature:

     wine w/5 label!

     This query yields far fewer documents. One of the documents returned is 27 USC§205. This is the Federal Alcohol Administration Act regarding unfair competition and unlawful practices. Subsection (e) sets labeling requirements.

Guided Exercise: Internet Searching

With Internet searching, strategy again leads the way. Avoid the research trap of searching the entire Web for something that is likely to be in one place. As you now know, agencies generally administer statutes.

1.   **Use the wine example in the preceding Guided Exercise. Answer this question: Which agency would you predict administers laws about wine labels?** (Feel free to browse the chart of federal agencies now on this text's Web site.) If you guessed the Food and Drug Administration, you are right.

2.   **Confirm your answer.** Access the Food and Drug Administration Web site. Try to make an educated guess to determine the site address—**http://www.fda.gov**.

3.   **Get ideas about how to search.** At the FDA Web site, take a moment to look at its search help section for ideas about how to search. You will see that the FDA uses Google to power its search, so the skills you have will fare you well. Try this query:

     wine and label and USC

     We added USC to the search because we want to be sure to get documents that have code citations in them. We know those documents will have the USC abbreviation, whereas they may not contain words like *statute* or *regulation*.

The search should yield several documents that discuss labeling requirements for wine, including relevant citations. The search results take advantage of the backward search strategy discussed earlier. By looking at secondary source material on the FDA Web site, we find both the relevant statute and information about its enforcement. This is much better information than we would find looking at the statute alone.

STATUTORY INTERPRETATION

Once you find your statute, you may need to determine its meaning. To do this, use the rules of statutory interpretation. The first rule of statutory interpretation is to look at the plain meaning of the statute, that is, ask yourself what the statute seems to mean on its face. As you can imagine, the plain meaning is not always so plain. The Federal Endangered Species Act is a good example. This law prevents the taking of an endangered species. Read the following statutory language:

> **16 USC 1538 Prohibited Acts....** *(W)ith respect to any endangered species of fish or wildlife listed pursuant to section 1533 of this title it is unlawful for any person subject to the jurisdiction of the United States to—*
>
> *(B)* ***take*** *any such species within the United States or the Territorial sea of the United States; ...*

You may ask what it means to take an endangered species. The plain meaning might lead you to believe that take means to pick up the species and remove it from its habitat. If so, you would be only partially correct. Thus, it is important that legal researchers not assume they know what important terms mean. So how can you determine what a word really means? Well, one step is to look at the legislation itself. Statutes frequently include definitions sections that explain the meanings of potentially confusing words.

> **16 USC 1532(19) Definitions.** *The term "take" means to harass, harm, pursue, hunt, shoot, wound, kill, trap, capture, or collect, or to attempt to engage in any such conduct.*

Another option is to look to the regulations related to the statute. They often contain definitions and explanations that clarify the statute. In this example, the Department of the Interior created regulatory definitions for the Endangered Species Act. These regulatory definitions are found in the Code of Federal Regulations.[4]

> **50 CFR § 17.3 Definitions.** *Harass in the definition of "take" in the Act means an intentional or negligent act or omission which creates the likelihood of injury to wildlife by annoying it to such an extent as to significantly disrupt normal behavioral patterns which include, but are not limited to, breeding, feeding, or sheltering. This definition, when applied to captive wildlife, does not include generally accepted:*
>
> *(1) Animal husbandry practices that meet or exceed the minimum standards for facilities and care under the Animal Welfare Act,*
>
> *(2) Breeding procedures, or*

(3) Provisions of veterinary care for confining, tranquilizing, or anesthetizing, when such practices, procedures, or provisions are not likely to result in injury to the wildlife.

Harm in the definition of "take" in the Act means an act which actually kills or injures wildlife. Such act may include significant habitat modification or degradation where it actually kills or injures wildlife by significantly impairing essential behavioral patterns, including breeding, feeding, or sheltering.

A third option is to look at case law, which may interpret the meaning of the confusing section as well. A little research on this issue reveals that the main case on this matter is *Babbit v Sweet Home*, 515 U.S. 687 (1995). In the *Babbit* case, the Sweet Home Chapter of Communities for a Great Oregon challenged the authority of the Secretary of the Department of the Interior to include the word *harm* in the definition of the word *take*. The United States Supreme Court confirmed that it was reasonable for the Secretary to create such a definition. In this excerpt from the case, the court looks at the legislative history for you.

Our conclusion that the Secretary's definition of "harm" rests on a permissible construction of the ESA gains further support from the legislative history of the statute. The Committee Reports accompanying the bills that became the ESA do not specifically discuss the meaning of "harm," but they make clear that Congress intended "take" to apply broadly to cover indirect as well as purposeful actions. The Senate Report stressed that "'take' is defined ... in the broadest possible manner to include every conceivable way in which a person can 'take' or attempt to 'take' any fish or wildlife." S. Rep. No. 93-307, p. 7 (1973). The House Report stated that "the broadest possible terms" were used to define restrictions on takings. H. R. Rep. No. 93-412, p. 15 (1973). The House Report underscored the breadth of the "take" definition by noting that it included "harassment, whether intentional or not." Id., at 11 (emphasis added).[5]

If you look at those three sources and still do not know what your confusing section means, it is time to turn to legislative history. **Legislative history** is a collection of documents that record the entire process of a bill's becoming law, from its first presentation to the legislature, through committee, to its final vote, to signing by the president or to the legislature's override of a veto. Given all this useful information, you may wonder why legislative history appears to be a last resort. The main reason is that researching legislative history can be complicated, confusing, and frustrating. Fortunately, the average researcher does not need to research legislative history very often. Because of that, this

legislative history
documentation of the process that a bill went through to become a law. Often used to interpret the law after its passage.

chapter does not discuss how to research legislative history. However, Appendix A contains more information on how to do it, including four simple steps to get started.

SUMMARY

Searching for statutes gives you the opportunity to use all your research skills. No matter what piece of information you have to begin with, you can find the relevant statute. After determining that a statute is really what you want and after confirming the appropriate jurisdiction, you can find statutes with a citation, the statute title, or a topic or keywords.

After finding your statute, you need to determine its meaning. Courts usually look first to the plain meaning of a statute, but actually understanding the meaning of a statute generally takes more than a simple reading of the law. Understanding simple rules of statutory interpretation can help you make initial determinations to aid your analysis.

NOTES

1. Statutes on FindLaw at **(http://www.findlaw.com/casecode)**.
2. Cornell Law School Statutes section at **(http://www.law.cornell. edu/uscode/)**.
3. You may also do this exercise by using Loislaw with slight modifications.
4. It is frequently believed that the Environmental Protection Agency is the lead agency on the Endangered Species Act. This is not the case. The U.S. Fish and Wildlife Service, a section of the Department of the Interior, maintains the list of more than 600 endangered species. For general information on the Endangered Species Program, visit **(http://endangered.fws.gov/)**.
5. *Babbit v Sweet Home*, 525 U.S. 687, p. 704 (1995).

EXERCISES

Chapter Review Exercises

Answer each of the following questions and include statutory citations to support your answers. Using the statute finding worksheets at the end of this chapter will help you find the appropriate statutes.

1. Our client, Pestly Pesticides, Inc., manufactures pesticides that are exported to Latin American countries. Which statute addresses whether the labels warning workers of the dangers of the product must be in English?

2. Allison Green is curious about what types of disabilities the Americans with Disabilities Act covers. What is the citation for that act?

3. Reading the local paper, Cheedy Jaja notices that the federal Department of Transportation recently held a meeting in his neighborhood regarding rail traffic. He wants to see the minutes and to read participants' testimony. He believes this is public information. Which statute would address whether the information is public?

4. Dissident Gavin Smith just finished his first novel, and he is convinced it will take the world by storm. He wants to copyright it, but he does not want the hassle of working with the government. Which statute addresses whether he needs to go through the Copyright Office to copyright the book?

Worksheet

Statute Finding Worksheet

Complete the worksheet before you begin your research process.
Starting information (fill in unknown information as you find it)
    Statute citation
    Statute name
    Statute topic/area of law

Initial questions
Is your statute state or federal?

What agency might administer this statute?

Are you sure that it is a statute that you are looking for? Why?

Tracking Information
From the keywords and other information you have, plot your strategy for finding the statute. What will be your first step and why? Complete this section of the worksheet before you actually begin the research, then record how it worked. (Do not worry if you do not take the exact number of steps listed in the worksheet—feel free to use the back of the worksheet to list more steps. If you can complete the task in fewer steps, celebrate your improved research skills!)

Step One:

Plan:

How Did It Work?

Step Two:

Plan:

How Did It Work?

Step Three:

Plan:

How Did It Work?

Step Four:

Plan:

How Did It Work?

Step Five:

Plan:

How Did It Work?

Worksheet

Statute Research Toolbox

Use this worksheet to comment on the Web sites listed and to include information on your favorites.

Website: Westlaw (**http://www.westlaw.com**)

Favorite features:

Comments:

Website: Lexis (**http://www.lexis.com**)

Favorite features:

Comments:

Website: Loislaw (**http://www.loislaw.com**)

Favorite features:

Comments:

Website: Food and Drug Administration (**http://www.fda.gov**)

Favorite features:

Comments:

Website: Legal Information Institute (**http://www.law.cornell.edu**)

Favorite features:

Comments:

Website: FindLaw (**http://www.findlaw.com**)

Favorite features:

Comments:

Finding and Understanding Regulations

CHAPTER

CHAPTER 6

CHAPTER OBJECTIVES

- **Review of administrative agencies:** What are regulations? Why you would look to them in legal research?

- **Review of the rule-making process:** Agencies go through a multi-step process to create regulations.

- **Regulation search strategy:** When searching for regulations, you start with certain pieces of information. In this chapter, you will explore how to find regulations when you have a citation, an agency name, a regulation name, or a topic.

- **Regulatory guidance search strategy:** Finding regulatory guidance for federal rules is quite manageable using a simple three-step process.

ON THE WEB

- http://www.paralegal.delmar.cengage.com
- Annotated links leading you to:
  - Federal and state regulations
  - More information on the regulatory process
  - Examples of agency guidance
- Exercises for additional help

REVIEW OF ADMINISTRATIVE AGENCIES

administrative agencies
a part of the executive branch, administrative agencies have the role of being experts in and advising on a particular area.

regulation
also known as a rule. Laws created by administrative agencies to implement statutes. A regulation must have statutory authority granted by the legislature.

rule-making
process of creating a rule or regulation. The Administrative Procedures Act (APA) sets out the multi-step process at the federal level.

rule
See regulation.

Federal Register
daily publication issued by the Government Printing Office that includes, among other things, notices on rule making.

guidance information
an administrative agency gives this information to help the regulated community comply with regulations.

codification
process of organizing laws according to subject.

Administrative agencies, part of the executive branch of government, are responsible for crafting **regulations**. Generally, only the legislative branch can create law. However, legislatures are able to delegate some lawmaking authority to administrative agencies.

Agencies create rules using a basic **rule-making** process. First a **rule** is proposed. Then the rule is published where people are likely to read it. At the federal level, that is the *Federal Register*. Many states also have publications for announcing proposed rules and other important state information. Publication of the proposed rule starts the public comment period. Interested parties can submit comments via letter or e-mail or in person at public meetings. Comment periods generally last from 30 to 60 days.

After interested parties submit comments, the agency reviews those comments and determines whether changes to the proposed rule are needed. If the agency makes major changes to the rule based on the comments, then the agency publishes the revised proposed rule and seeks additional comments. If changes are minor, then the agency simply publishes the final rule. Often a lengthy explanation of the rule's background and how the agency anticipates enforcing it accompanies publication of the final rule. This explanation is known as **guidance**, which this chapter discusses later.

After a final rule is published, it is eventually **codified**. At the federal level, the rule becomes part of the Code of Federal Regulations (C.F.R.). At the state level, names vary, with some states having different codes for different agencies. This chapter focuses on finding codified regulations at the state and federal level.

REGULATION SEARCH STRATEGY

Generally, when you need to look for a regulation, you begin with one or more of the following pieces of information:

- citation
- agency name
- regulation name
- topic

Let's explore the strategies used to find regulations by using each one of these pieces of information.

Finding a Regulation with a Citation

Ideally, you will have a full citation to work with. This is the easiest way to search for information. A citation from the Code of Federal Regulations provides an example. 40 C.F.R. 1501.4 explains the criteria that the Environmental Protection Agency should use to determine whether to conduct an environmental impact statement.

Regulation with Citation on Westlaw

Finding a federal regulation with a citation on Westlaw could not be simpler. Speed your work by omitting the periods in C.F.R.—Westlaw does not need them to find your citation. You can do this quick search for federal or state materials.

Instructions: To use Find this Document by Citation to find a statute by citation, follow these steps:

1. Go to the Find this Document by Citation search box on the main page of Westlaw.
2. Enter your citation in the search box and click on the Go button.
3. If you have trouble pulling up your desired document, check the Help section to ensure you entered your citation correctly.

Regulation with Citation on Lexis

You can find federal regulations easily using Lexis's Get a Document feature. When entering your citation, remember that you do not need to enter periods, section signs, or other symbols in the citation box. Get a Document works for both state and federal citations.

Instructions: To use Get a Document to find a regulation by citation, follow these steps:

1. Click on Get a Document on the tab at the top of the screen.
2. You have three choices on the left: Citation, Party Name, and Docket Number. Choose Citation.
3. Enter your citation in the search box and click on the Get button.
4. If you have trouble pulling up your desired document, check the Citation Formats link next to the Citation search box to ensure you entered your citation correctly.

Regulation with Citation on Loislaw

Loislaw makes it easy to find documents with a citation as long as you know which jurisdiction you are working in.

Instructions: To find a regulation with a citation in Loislaw, follow these steps:

1. Click on the Admin. Rules & Regulations database
2. Select the jurisdiction (specific state or federal) that you want to search. You can select multiple jurisdictions if you are unsure of the correct one. Click on Continue at the bottom of the page.

3. Enter your citation in the Heading section of the search page.
4. If you have trouble pulling up your desired document, check the Help section to ensure that you used the correct citation format.

Regulation with Citation on Casemaker

Casemaker makes it easy to find documents with a citation, but be certain to use the correct citation format.

Instructions: To find a regulation with a citation in Casemaker, follow these steps:

1. In Casemaker, access your state library.
2. Choose your state's regulation library by clicking on the Search button. (Note that some states do not have the search feature available. Simply use the Browse button to step through the regulatory code to your specific citation.)
3. When you get the search box, click on the Advanced Search tab.
4. Enter your citation in the Citation search box. Check to confirm that any options for the type of citation you are entering have been selected.
5. If you have trouble pulling up your desired document, check the Help section to ensure that you used the correct citation format.

Regulation with Citation on the Internet

You can use a variety of strategies to find regulations on the Internet. One option is to just put your citation in the search box of your favorite Web site like Google (**http://www.google.com**) or All The Web (**http://www.alltheweb.com**). Another way is to visit a Web site that offers a selection of regulations. FindLaw (**http://www.findlaw.com**) and the Cornell Law School Web site (**http://law.cornell.edu**) are two good choices, because they include both state and federal citations. Both Cornell and FindLaw lead you to state Web pages with state regulations if the regulations are available on the Internet. For just federal regulations, use the Web site of the Government Printing Office (**http://www.gpoaccess.gov**). This Web site also includes access to the *Federal Register*, which provides explanatory information about federal regulations.

Whether looking state or federal regulatory citations, you can also browse for the regulation, especially if you have only a portion of the citation. This feature is generally available under a Table of Contents heading. If you find your title and section that way, they may lead you to what you want.

Another strategy for searching for regulations by citation on the Internet is to visit the Web page of the particular agency, if you know which agency you need. Many agencies at both the state and federal levels post their regulations on their Web sites in both searchable and

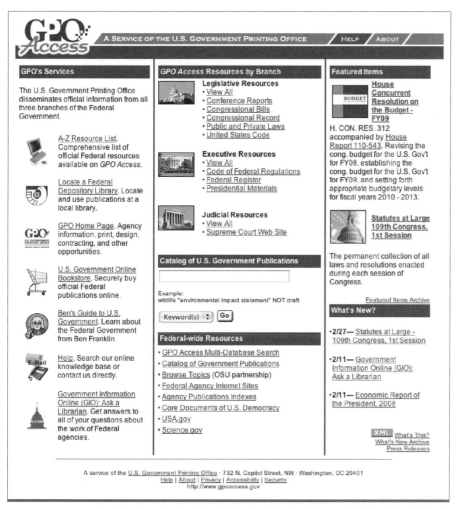

Exhibit 6–1 The Code of Federal Regulations is available on the website of the Government Printing Office.

Source: From (**http://www.gpoaccess.gov**)

browsable formats. The advantage of finding your regulation on the agency Web site is that agencies often have general explanations of the regulations in plain English, designed for the **regulated community**. This can be especially useful to the researcher, particularly if you are unfamiliar with the specific regulation at hand.

For our example, 40 CFR 1501.4, the Environmental Protection Agency is the issuing agency. Go to the EPA Web site (**http://www. epa.gov**), and select Laws, Regulations and Dockets. Then select the Code of Federal Regulations link. You can choose the entire CFR or just Title 40. Following our general rule of selecting the narrowest database, select the Title 40 link and go to the link that includes Part 1501.

regulated community
businesses and individuals subject to an agency's regulations.

Exercise
6-1

Look up the following regulations by their citations, using at least two different databases for comparison purposes.

1. 45 CFR 702.5
2. 36 CFR 1150.13
3. 16 CFR 1502.16
4. GA COMP. R. & REGS. 300-2-5-.02 (Georgia)
5. Minn. R. 9500.1463 (Minnesota)
6. 10 NMAC 5.100.8 (New Mexico)

Summarize your research experience by answering the following questions:

a. Which two databases did you use?
b. Overall, which database seemed the most easy to use?
c. What were the advantages of the easier database?
d. What were the disadvantages of the more challenging database?

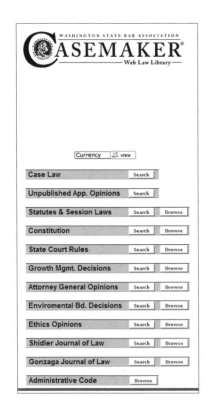

Exhibit 6–2 Casemaker Table of Contents.

Source: From (**http://www.casemaker.us**)

Finding a Regulation with an Agency Name

If you have no citation, but you have a subject and an agency name, you can visit the agency's Web site. Many agencies, both at the state and the federal levels, post their regulations on their Web pages along with great explanatory information. As long as you have a topic, you can browse your way to what you need.

Finding a Regulation with Its Name

If you have the name of the regulation, your best bet may be to type that name into the search box of your favorite Internet search engine. Chances are that the full text of your regulation will be within your first 10 hits.

If you cannot find the information using a general Web search, try a more specific database search. Be aware that using a specific database to search for a set of regulations by name can sometimes be pretty frustrating. The problem is that every single section of a regulation has a heading that contains the regulation's name. If you are fortunate and your regulation has only a few sections, you should have no trouble. More often than not, though, a regulation has dozens of sections. Using the handy Table of Contents feature is simpler, if one is available. The Table of Contents feature makes online searching more like using a book, giving you the best of both worlds. You can use the Table of Contents feature to find your citation, or you can use it as an information-gathering tool, a guide to narrowing the results of a more general search. However, if you have the regulation's name and a keyword, you can probably use a general search tool more effectively.

Find a citation for the following regulations. Remember to use all your research skills when doing this exercise. Do not forget the skills and tools that you learned in the earlier chapters.

1. Food and Drug Administration enforcement policies (federal)
2. Legal Services Corporation appeals on behalf of clients (federal)
3. Fish and Wildlife Service Proceedings for seizure and forfeiture of wildlife (federal)
4. Arizona Department of Agriculture rules on parlors and milk rooms
5. Maryland Childcare Administration requirements for the home
6. Wyoming Crime Victims Compensation Commission Profits from Crime

Finding a Regulation with a Topic

Sometimes you need to search for a regulation when you have only a topic to start with. If that is the case, you can try two different approaches. Start the easy way and do a general Internet search using your topic and the regulation code abbreviation. For example, in Google, try the following query to find federal statutes about education.

Education CFR

Note that Google defaults to the AND operator, so there is no need to include it in our query. You should find the relevant information within your first five results.

If you know the agency that administers the regulation, you could search directly using the agency's Web site. As mentioned previously, using the agency Web site will lead you not only to your specific regulation, but will also likely have supporting documents to help you understand what the regulation means and how it is implemented.

You can also do this search in a paid legal database, using your keyword and selecting your specific regulatory directory. Using our previous example, you would find the Code of Federal Regulations directory and search the word *Education*. Narrow your search by using Westlaw's Locate feature or Lexis' Focus feature.

If you have only a topic, and you are not certain of the **jurisdiction**, your search is even more challenging. The best thing to do is to ask the person who assigned you the question (i.e., your teacher or supervising attorney) for more jurisdictional information. If that doesn't work, you can use a few different approaches.

First, use common sense to narrow the jurisdiction as much as possible. Remember that states tend to address some topics (like family law) and other topics tend to fall under federal jurisdiction. If your topic does

jurisdiction

as referred to in this chapter, indicates whether a regulation falls under state or federal law.

not neatly fall into one category or another (like environmental law), you will need to try a broader approach.

The most effective broad approach might be a general Internet search. Include the terms *regulation* or *rule* or possibly *agency* to narrow the results to more relevant hits. You could also do this with a general search on a paid legal database. If doing so, remember that regulations, like statutes, use specific terms in particular ways; if you don't select just the right term, your search may not succeed. One option to get around this limit is to search cases for regulations. Cases often use more general language and also cite directly to the relevant regulation.

Effective regulatory searches are based on the information you have available. By figuring out what you have and combining the methods described here, you can find regulations quickly, no matter what information you start with.

Exercise 6-3

1. Find one regulation to answer each of the following questions regarding federal regulations.
   a. Is it fair practice to use secret coding in market research dealing with silk?
   b. What is the purpose of the Amateur Radio Service?
   c. What is involved in a space-shuttle rendezvous?

2. Find your state's regulations on the following topics. Answer the questions, supporting your answers with the appropriate citations.
   a. Find your state's regulations on getting a license to practice law. Who is eligible?
   b. Find your state's regulations on food safety. What is required to get a food handler's card?
   c. Find your state's regulations on transportation. Do they include traffic regulations for bicycling?

REGULATORY GUIDANCE SEARCH STRATEGY

After you find your regulations, you might need to figure out what they mean. If that is the case, turn to regulatory guidance for help. Regulatory guidance consists mainly of comments that accompany the rules at various stages of publication. In that way, it is similar to legislative history but fortunately much easier to access and understand. Some agencies also publish separate guidance or policy documents specifically for the purpose of clarifying confusing rules or explaining the rules' enforcement. Another source of regulatory guidance is agency correspondence written in response to formal requests for regulatory interpretation from members of the regulated community. These combined sources can go a long way toward explaining the meaning of an unclear

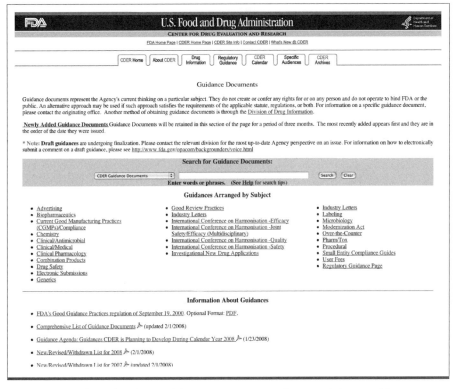

Exhibit 6–3 FDA Guidance. Many agencies make regulatory guidance available online.

Source: From (**http://www.fda.gov**)

regulation. As mentioned earlier, finding regulatory guidance is relatively simple compared to finding legislative history. The next section lists the steps that should start you on your way.

Finding Regulatory Guidance

To find most federal regulatory guidance, follow this simple three-step formula:

1. Find the regulation.
2. Look up the relevant *Federal Register* notices.
3. Look for other sources of guidance.

The next section discusses these steps in detail. Remember, this three-step process is designed for research at the federal level. Steps for finding your state's guidance vary, depending on the process your state uses. Many states publish state registers that contain information similar to the *Federal Register*. Thus, the steps described here should be useful in leading you to state guidance as well.

Guided Exercise

Follow these steps to learn the simple procedure you can use to find regulatory guidance.

1. **Find the regulation.** The first step to understanding what any legal document means is to have that document in front of you. Like statutes, regulations end with valuable information that leads you to the information you need. The National Poultry Improvement Plan, located at 9 CFR 145, *et seq.* offers a good example. The next steps look specifically at the general provisions at 9 CFR 145.4.

Exhibit 6–4 Logo for National Poultry Improvement Plan.

Source: From the Code of Federal Regulations, 9 CFR 145.4.

2. **Look up the *Federal Register* notices.** At least two *Federal Register* notices are associated with each rule—the proposed rule and the final rule. Quite likely, several more notices are available as well. Look up and read them all. Finding *Federal Register* notices with the citation is easy; you can get the citations at the end of the regulation.

   In our example, 9 CFR 145.4 lists seven *Federal Register* citations (abbreviated as FR). Can you determine which notice relates to the proposed rule? To the final rule? Look up your answers to see if they are right. Hint: Generally, the first notice listed is the proposed rule, and the second notice is the final rule. There are, of course, many exceptions. You can also use a process of elimination to determine which notices are proposed and which are final. If the notation says *as amended* or *redesignated at*, you know those are changes to the rule, not the original rule.

3. **Look for other sources of guidance.** Though the *Federal Register* is the most easily accessible source of federal regulatory guidance, agencies provide guidance in other ways as well. This alternate guidance generally takes the form of specially written guidance documents, policy statements, opinions, and answers to written questions from the regulated community. You can find all of this information on specific agency Web sites.

Each agency does things slightly differently, of course. As you become familiar with individual agencies, you will become familiar with how each agency shares its vision of how to do things. If you are unfamiliar with the agency from which you are seeking guidance, the best place to start is the agency's Web page. Online, agencies tend to keep their guidance in the same place they keep their regulations, so look for that on the agency home page. Alternatively, search for the words *policy* or *guidance* by using the agency's internal search engine.

For our example of the National Poultry Improvement Plan, the appropriate agency is the United States Department of Agriculture (**http://www.usda.gov**). Visit the agency's Web site, and see if you can find additional information about the National Poultry Improvement Plan. Hint: Search the Web site by using a phrase search for the regulation title. Remember to check the search help to ensure you are using the proper phrase search technique.

Keep an open mind when looking for agency guidance. It can come in many forms: an official document with the title "Agency Guidance," a penalty policy, a formal letter to a member of the regulated community, or an informative brochure on how to comply with the regulation. Any information from the agency that helps you understand the rule and how to comply with it can be categorized as agency guidance.

Look on the following agency Web sites, and find examples of agency guidance. Note the title of at least one guidance document you find.

1. Department of Transportation (**http://www.dot.gov**)
2. Federal Trade Commission (**http://www.ftc.gov**)
3. Food and Drug Administration (**http://www.fda.gov**)

Exercise 6-4

Personal Contacts

Each *Federal Register* notice contains contact information for a specific federal employee who is an expert on the regulation noted. The contact person may know more about your regulation than anyone else, because they are often personally involved with the rulemaking from the beginning. Don't hesitate to call or e-mail the contact person and ask questions—they can be extremely helpful.

SUMMARY

Researching regulations is a fairly straightforward process when you are searching electronically. Your search strategy depends on what information you start with. Whether you have the citation, the agency name, the regulation name, or just a topic to work with, you can use that information to find a regulation.

Once you find the regulation, you may be interested in interpreting it. If so, you can investigate agency guidance. Finding guidance is also a relatively straightforward task. Look up the relevant regulation and its register notices, and you will be well on your way to finding useful information about implementing the law.

EXERCISES

Chapter Review Exercises:

1. The following queries have different types of information for federal regulations. Figure out what you have, determine a strategy, and find the answers to the questions.

   a. How does the Food and Drug Administration define French dressing?

   b. What is the Literacy Leader Fellowship Program?

   c. What does 22 CFR 1508.100 discuss?

   d. What is the regulatory citation for the hearing procedures for the Merchant Marine Act?

   e. What does 45 CFR 1605.1 discuss?

2. Using a favorite news source or an agency's Web site, find a recently finalized regulation, and answer the following questions about it. Support your answers with citations to your sources.

   a. What is the citation of the regulation, and what statute authorizes it?

   b. Why did the agency write the regulation?

   c. Was there much comment during the public comment period? Did the agency modify the proposed rule as a result?

   d. Who does the new regulation impact?

Worksheet

Federal Register Location Worksheet

Source: Westlaw
Location: Under the Federal Materials heading, select Administrative Rules and Regulations to find several options for the *Federal Register* (FR), including the Table of Contents feature and an organization by practice area.
Comments:

Source: Lexis
Location: Under Federal Legal, select *FR - Federal Register.*
Comments:

Source: Loislaw
Location: Select the Administrative Rules and Regulations database and then select *Federal Register.*
Comments:

Source: Casemaker
Location: Does not have the *Federal Register.*
Comments:

Source: Internet
Location: The Government Printing Office maintains the *Federal Register* online. (**http://gpoaccess.gov/fr**) The database dates back to 1995.
Comments:

Worksheet

Regulation Finding Worksheet

Complete as much of the worksheet as you can before you begin researching.
Starting information: Fill in unknown information as you find it.

Regulation citation:
Regulation name:
Regulation topic/area of law:

Initial Questions

Is it state or federal?

What agency might administer this regulation?

Am I sure that I am looking for a regulation? Why?

Tracking Information: From the keywords and other information you have, plot your strategy for finding the regulation. What will be your first step and why? Complete this section of the worksheet before you actually begin the research, then record how your research worked. (Do not worry if you do not take the exact number of steps listed in the worksheet—feel free to use the back of the worksheet to list more steps. If you can complete the task in fewer steps, celebrate your improved research skills!)

Step One:

Plan:

How Did It Work?

Step Two:

Plan:

How Did It Work?

Step Three:

Plan:

How Did It Work?

Step Four:

Plan:

How Did It Work?

Step Five:

Plan:

How Did It Work?

Worksheet

Regulation Research Toolbox

Use this chart to comment on the Web sites listed and to include information on your favorites.

Web site: Westlaw (**http://www.westlaw.com**)

Favorite features:

Comments:

Web site: Lexis (**http://www.lexis.com**)

Favorite features:

Comments:

Web site: Loislaw (**http://www.loislaw.com**)

Favorite features:

Comments:

Web site: FirstGov (**http://www.firstgov.gov**)

Favorite features:

Comments:

Web site: Government Printing Office (**http://www.gpoaccess.gov**)

Favorite Features:

Comments:

Web site: US Department of Agriculture (**http://www.usda.gov**)

Favorite features:

Comments:

Web site:

Favorite features:

Comments:

Web site:

Favorite features:

Comments:

Web site:

Favorite features:

Comments:

Finding Cases

CHAPTER 7

CHAPTER OBJECTIVES

- **Review case law:** Finding cases online is quicker and easier than using books.
- **Learn strategies for searching case law:** When searching for cases, you will learn to find cases when you have a citation, party names, or a topic.

ON THE WEB

- http://www.paralegal.delmar.cengage.com
- Annotated links leading you to:
  - U.S. Supreme Court case archives
  - State and federal cases online
- Exercises for extra help

REVIEW OF CASE LAW

Case law is created primarily in appellate courts. You have undoubtedly studied the structure of the court system, and your understanding of it is of foremost importance when doing case research. If you are confused about the structure of the courts and the name of each level, you might be unable to make much progress in electronic case research. Indeed, you might not realize whether a case meets your needs if you do not understand where the case came from and its impact on other courts.

Check the end of this chapter for a handy chart (Table 7–3) with the structure of the federal courts. In Table 7–4, you can enter your state court information. With this information, you are ready to begin your electronic search for case law.

CASE LAW SEARCH STRATEGY

Generally, when you need to look for a case, you start with at least one piece of information: a citation, party names, or a topic. The next sections look at the different research strategies that you might use.

Exhibit 7–1 A good research strategy is essential.

Finding a Case with a Citation

A citation makes your search for case law quick and easy. Most paid legal databases have a place, separate from the ordinary search box, where you can simply enter the citation and find your case. This is true whether you are using Westlaw, Lexis, or Loislaw. When using Westlaw or Lexis, updating your citation on the spot is also simple using Shepards, KeyCite, or Global Cite. That is a great habit to get into, because far too often, legal researchers neglect the important step of updating their primary law.

Duty to Check Your Cite

As a legal researcher, you have a duty to **cite check.** Cite checking, also known as Shepardizing, is the process of verifying the accuracy and validity of your citations to make sure they are still good law. There are dozens of cases in which the court chastised attorneys for not checking their cites and thus missing some otherwise obvious information. Cite checking is easy to skip, but doing so can lead to embarrassment and potential liability for your firm.

cite checking
see Shepardizing

When looking for cases with the citation, you must be careful about how you enter the citation.

- Use basic *Bluebook* form, although you generally do not have to include periods or spacing, which will save you a few keystrokes.
- You do not need to enter party names, dates, or parallel citations.
- Do not spell out abbreviations or create your own.
- Make a point to check the Help section for the abbreviation protocol of the resources you choose.

Bluebook, a uniform system of citation
style guide with a uniform system of citation. A small book with a blue cover, the *Bluebook* is used by most legal professionals for proper citation format.

All of these practices help you avoid the frustration of entering a good citation but not finding any cases.

Guided Exercises

Table 7–1 lists the main research resources discussed in this text and provides abbreviated formats for citations. Look up the following citations. Use at least one paid legal database and one Internet resource. Use more resources if you have access to them.

(continued)

a. *Ducolon Mechanical, Inc. v Shinstine/Forness, Inc.*, 77 Wash. App. 707, 893 P.2d 1127 (1995)

b. *Bank v Truck Ins. Exch.*, 51 F.3d 736 (7th Cir. 1995)

c. *State v Chang*, 587 N.W.2d 459 (Iowa 1997)

parallel citation
second location for the same case. For example, a case might be found both in a state reporter and the regional reporter.

You may notice that the format varies from source to source. *Note:* As a general rule of efficiency, if you have a **parallel citation**, you should enter the one with fewer characters. Usually you can enter either one of the citations to find the case. See Table 7–1 for an example of citation abbreviation styles for cases.

Table 7–1: Abbreviation format for case law

Resource	Format	Comments
Westlaw	a. 77 wash app 707 b. 51 f3d 736 c. 587 nw 2d 459	No need to use capital letters or periods. The spacing included here is also unnecessary—you can run numbers and letters together.
Lexis	a. 77 wash app 707 b. 51 f3d 736 c. 587 nw 2d 459	No need to use capital letters or periods.
Loislaw	a. 77 wash app 707 b. 51 f3d 736 c. 587 nw 2d 459	Be careful with citation format. Use strict *Bluebook* format.
CaseMaker	a. NA b. NA c. NA	
FindLaw	a. 77 wn app 707 b. 51 f3d 736 c. 587 nw 2d 459	Be sure to use the phrase searching quotation marks and to use *Bluebook* format. Also, be certain you are using the "all legal websites" option to get the best results.
Legal Information Institute	a. NA b. NA c. NA	The Cornell Law School site stores few of its own cases. Instead, it connects you to other Web sites. You'll want to check those Web sites for the best way to cite. You may need to have the decision date, docket number, or party names.

Exercise 7–1

Find the names of the following cases and answer the related question. Use one or more search tools so that you can compare results.

1. Was the applicant denied due process? 57 F.Supp.2d. 1305 (1999)
2. Whose duty is it to engage in prosecutorial discretion? 127 N.M. 566, 985 P.2d 168 (1999)

(continued)

Exercise 7–1

3. Under Minnesota law, how should contractual provisions be interpreted? 186 F.3d 981 (1999)
4. What does a plaintiff have to demonstrate to get a preliminary injunction? 673 N.Y.S.2d 450, 242 A.D.2d 52 (1998)
5. What is the precise and universal test of relevancy? 48 Conn. App. 717, 711 A.2d 769 (1998)
6. When should the *per se* rule be applied? 143 F.3d 914 (1998)

Finding a Case with Party Names

Searching with party names is relatively straightforward if you are aware of a couple of things. First, depending on where and how you search, you may get back several results with the same party names. Those results might include earlier decisions in lower courts, rehearings of the same case, or denials of *certiorari* by the court of last resort. If you have information in addition to party names, such as the reporter or date, quickly searching the results for that information is easy and may help you find what you want. If not, do not be afraid to actually open the cases to see if one meets your needs.

Here is another thing to remember when you search for party names: You do not always need to enter both names. For example, criminal cases have *State* or *People* as the **plaintiff**. That means that the government is suing on behalf of the people. Because the government files thousands of cases every year, entering *State* or *People* as the party name is not likely to enhance your results. Try just entering the **defendant's** name. For example, for the case *State v Brandemies*, just enter the party name *Brandemies*.

For common party names, such as Smith or Jones, make use of any other information you have. For example, many databases let you use date restrictions. If you know the year of the decision, you can use it to limit your results. So a party name search for the case *State v Smith* might find many cases in addition to the one you want. If you can, also include the jurisdiction, dates, and docket number to narrow the results.

The next sections include some database-specific information.

Case with Party Names on Westlaw

In Westlaw, once you have selected your database, you can do a field restricted search to search only the party names.

Instructions: To find a case with party names in Westlaw, follow these steps.

1. From the home page, look for Find a Document by Title, near the Find a Document By Citation box.
2. Enter the party names in the appropriate boxes.

plaintiff
person who sues at the trial court level.

defendant
party who is being sued at the trial court level.

Case with Party Names on Lexis

In Lexis, there are two ways to search with party name. The easiest is to use the Get a Document option.

Instructions: To use Get a Document to find a case by party name:

- Click on Get a Document by using the tab at the top of the screen.
- You have three choices on the left: Citation, Party Name, and Docket Number. Choose Party Name.
- Enter your party name(s) in the appropriate box(es) and click on the Get button.

Case with Party Names on Loislaw

In Loislaw, you need to be a bit more certain of what you are looking for. First, you must be fairly specific when selecting a database. For example, Loislaw has separate databases for state appellate and state supreme court decisions. If you do not know the court level, remember that you can select multiple databases to search. Simply select the ones that seem most likely to yield results. You can also select all of the relevant databases if you are uncertain of the correct one to choose.

Once you select the database, you can enter the party names on the appellant/appellee or plaintiff/defendant line.

Instructions: To find a case with party names in Loislaw, follow these steps.

1. In Loislaw, click on the Case Law database.
2. Select the jurisdiction (specific state or federal) that you want to search. You can select multiple jurisdictions if you are unsure of the correct one. Click on Continue at the bottom of the page.
3. Enter the party names on the case name line.

Another useful tool in Loislaw is the NEAR operator. Use it in the basic search box. By entering the party names, separated by the NEAR# operator (with a relatively small number such as 2 or 3), you should be able to reduce the number of irrelevant results.[1] For example, you might enter the query:

Delahunty NEAR3 morgan

You will find that query an effective way to search for a party name using the basic search box.

Case with Party Names in Casemaker

In Casemaker, you can easily do a search for party names by using the Advanced Search box.

Instructions: To find a case with party names in Casemaker, follow these steps.

1. In Casemaker, access your state library.
2. Choose the case law library for your state or the federal one.
3. When you get the search box, click on the Advanced Search tab.
4. Enter your party names in the Citation search box. Click on the Case Name radio button to properly limit the search.

Case with Party Names on the Internet

You can also use the Internet to search by party name. You could put the party names in Google or the search engine of your choice. If you choose a Web site such as Cornell's Legal Information Institute, then the method is quite similar to party name searches on paid legal databases. Be aware of the types of search boxes for entering the party names. If the site has a box for each name, you can enter one party name in each box. If not, you could enter something such as *Smith v Jones* in a search box. You might also want to try a search using the familiar Boolean search operators, with a query such as:

Smith AND Jones
or
Smith NEAR Jones

Be Aware the Date of the Case

The sample cases presented in this text are all fairly recent. Generally, it is much easier to find recent law (the early 1990s onward) online. Older cases are being added all the time. However, if you can't find an older case, it could be that the case just is not available for free online.

Guided Exercises

Table 7–2 lists the main sources discussed in this text and provides formats for names. Look at the following citations. Using the information in Table 7–2, determine the names. Use at least one paid legal database and one Internet site.

Note how the format varies from source to source, as illustrated in Table 7–2.

a. *People of California v Halaliku Kaloni Tufunga*, 21 Cal. 4th 935, 987 P. 2d 168 (1999)

b. *Marshall Dominguez v Paul Davidson*, 266 Kan. 296, 974 P.2d 112 (1999)

c. *Carol Kolstad v American Dental Association*, 527 US 526 (1999)
See Table 7–2 for examples of how to enter case names.

(continued)

Table 7–2: Abbreviation format for party names

Source	Format	Comments
Westlaw	**a.** Tufunga **b.** Dominguez & Davidson **c.** Kolstad & ADA	a. With unusual party names, if you select the proper jurisdiction, you can enter just one name to find the case successfully. b. If you choose to use both party names, use the "&" between the party names. c. Shorten long names with appropriate abbreviations.
Lexis	**a.** Tufunga **b.** Dominguez (in the second space) Davidson **c.** Kolstad (and optionally in the second space), ADA	a. With unusual party names, you can just select the right jurisdiction and enter one name, and you should get the case. b. If you choose to use both party names, join them with AND. c. Shorten long names with appropriate abbreviations.
Loislaw	**a.** Tufunga **b.** Dominguez & Davidson **c.** Kolstad & American Dental Association	a. Using the California State case database, you need only one name to find this case. b. Use either AND or its symbol (&) to join the party names when using more than one. c. Using the *ADA* abbreviation yielded no results in this search. Spell long party names. However, you do not need a phrase connector to get accurate results.
Casemaker	**a.** Tufunga **b.** Dominguez Davidson **c.** Kolstad	a. Casemaker does not currently have a California database. b. The space between the party names is the equivalent of the AND connector. c. Using the *ADA* abbreviation yielded no results in this search. Spell out long party names or omit and do a single name search.
FindLaw	**a.** Tufunga **b.** Dominguez Davidson **c.** Kolstad	a. Using the California State case database, only one name was needed to find the case. b. Using AND or v yielded no results. Simply enter the party names. c. FindLaw instructions suggest entering only one party name.
Legal Information Institute	**a.** Tufunga **b.** Dominguez (and in the second line) Davidson	a. Simply entering this unique party name in the search box yielded an accurate result as the second hit. b. Select the highest court when you are uncertain of

(continued)

c. Kolstad

the jurisdiction. Use Advanced Search whenever you can. Using it here allowed for a title (party name) search.

c. Entering this unique party name in the Quick Search box of the Supreme Court Collection brought the desired case as the first hit.

Use the following party name and jurisdictional information to answer the following questions. Include full citations in your answers. Try using a variety of resources to answer the questions.

1. What is the four-part test for determining whether injunctive relief should be granted? *Doe v Fauver* (D.N.J.1997)
2. What impact do "fighting words" have? *Lundgren v State* (Ga.App.1999)
3. If it looks like a criminal defendant might be insane, who in Massachusetts bears the burden of disproving that? *Commonwealth v Federici* (Mass 1998)
4. What does this Michigan court think about expert testimony regarding the credibility of a witness? *Franzel v Kerr Manufacturing Company* (Mich.App.1999)
5. When is extrinsic evidence admissible to determine the grantors intent in an easement? *Perillo v Credendino* (N.Y.A.D. 2 Dept 1999)
6. When should expert testimony be excluded? *Bryant v Buerman* (Fla. App. 4 Dist 1999)

Finding a Case with a Topic

Searching for case law electronically with a topic is much like doing any other topic search. It may help to recall the Boolean search strategies and the Five Questions described earlier in this text.

The main difference between general topic searches and searching for cases by topic is the database you select. Focusing on the appropriate case database puts you on the right track.

Searching by name and citation produces fairly limited results. However, topic searching is likely to provide dozens if not hundreds of results.

Case with Topic on Westlaw and Lexis

If your Westlaw or Lexis search finds too many documents, you can narrow your results by using the Westlaw Locate tool or the Lexis Focus tool. Those tools enable you to search the results of your current search.

This is a great help if your initial search is on the right track but yields too many results to work with efficiently.

- Look for Westlaw's Locate in Result link at the top of your results page, next to the Search button.
- Look for Lexis's Focus tool at the top of your results page.

You should search using the narrowest possible database. The Locate and Focus tools let you search the relatively small database of your current search results, so you can pinpoint your results even more. See the Lexis and Westlaw manuals for more information on how the tools work.

Case with Topic on Loislaw and Casemaker

In Loislaw and Casemaker, you can do topic searches by using the regular search box.

- In Loislaw, be sure to use the "search entire document" line at the top of the screen.
- In Casemaker, it is fine to use the default Basic search.

Additionally, several basic strategies that work in Lexis and Westlaw will work in other databases such as Loislaw and Casemaker as well. For example, you can narrow your search using the narrowest possible database and by using additional keywords.

Case with Topic on the Internet

When you do a topic case search on the Internet, the same tools you used in earlier chapters serve you well. You could do a global search on a tool such as Google or you could select a law-specific Web site to do your search. You will probably find using a law specific Web site will be more effective, because your global search will pull up all kinds of documents, not just cases. The temptation for many students is to include the word *case* in their query. However, remember that a search looks for terms in a document and many cases do not actually include the word *case*.

If you decided to search on a law-specific Web site, the same sites mentioned earlier, including FindLaw and the Legal Information Institute, are useful here as well. Take a moment to check how far back the cases on that Web site date before conducting your search. Also take a moment to look at the search criterion to make sure your query will be effective.

**Exercise
7–3**

Use case law to answer the following questions. There is not necessarily one right answer for each. Just try to find a case that accurately answers each question. Try using a variety of resources to answer the questions. (You might recall these questions from Chapter 1.)

1. Did Dick slander Jane when he wrote and published a truthful editorial about her bad housekeeping?
2. Is Lars liable for fraud because he sold stock for a company that did not exist?
3. Did Henry breach his contract with Luis when Henry delivered fresh flowers a day late, when time was of the essence?
4. Did Zora make a valid will when she left her entire estate to her cat, Mr. Pipo?
5. Is Badco liable for discrimination when it refuses to hire female workers over the age of 24?

SUMMARY

Whether you have a citation, party names, a topic, or a combination of these, finding a case is a fairly straightforward task. You can search effectively using any of the electronic resources discussed in this chapter. Remember this one limitation: Cases on the Internet tend to be more recent. However, most Web sites tell you the date range of cases on the search screen, so you can easily learn what is available.

The ease of searching for cases is fortunate, because cases are also a great way to find statutes and regulations, as discussed in Chapters 5 and 6. You might find that case law research is the type of research you do most.

For additional resources, please go to http://www.paralegal.delmar.cengage.com

CHAPTER REVIEW EXERCISES

Answer the following questions by using the information provided. Try to use at least two different search tools and compare their effectiveness. Comparisons can help you expand your research toolbox, enabling you to research more effectively in the future.

1. Kate's cat regularly enters Callie's yard to use the garden as a litter box. Can Callie sue Kate for the tort of trespass?

2. What is the general legal subject covered in the case located at 900 P.2d 113 (1995)?

3. Can Melody sue Off Note Records for using her copyrighted song without her permission?

4. What elements are needed to show intentional infliction of emotional distress?

5. What type of damages did Lord's and Lady's Enterprises, Inc. get in their 1999 case heard in the Massachusetts Appeals Court?

6. Deneen Sweeting was a defendant in the third circuit in 2000. What aspect of criminal law is his case about?

Table 7–3

Name of Court	Court Level	Case Reporter	Abbreviation
Federal District Court	Trial Court	Federal Supplement	F. Supp.
United States Court of Appeals	Appellate Court	Federal Reporter	F., F.2d, F.3d
United States Supreme Court	Appellate Court of last resort	United States Reports, Supreme Court Reporter Lawyer's Edition	U.S., S.Ct., L.Ed.

Now, fill in the same information for the courts in your state.

Table 7–4

Name of Court	Court Level	Case Reporter	Abbreviation

Worksheet

New Database Worksheet

Use this worksheet to record the relevant search information you discover when you explore new databases.

Database:

_____

Boolean Search:

_____

Proximity Search:

_____

Phrase Search:

_____

Stemming:

_____

Wildcard:

Worksheet

Case Research Toolbox

Use this chart to comment on the Web sites listed and to include information on your favorites.

Web site: Westlaw (**http://www.westlaw.com**)

Favorite Features:

Comments:

Web site: Lexis (**http://www.lexis.com**)

Favorite Features:

Comments:

Web site: Loislaw (**http://www.loislaw.com**)

Favorite Features:

Comments:

Web site: Google (http://www.google.com)

Favorite Features:

Comments:

Web site: FindLaw (**http://www.findlaw.com**)

Favorite Features:

Comments:

Web site: Legal Information Institute (**http://www.law.cornell.edu**)

Favorite Features:

Comments:

Web site:

Favorite Features:

Comments:

Web site:

Favorite Features:

Comments:

Web site:

Favorite Features:

Comments:

Web site:

Favorite Features:

Comments:

Finding Secondary Sources

CHAPTER 8

CHAPTER OBJECTIVES

- **Use dictionaries and encyclopedias:** Students generally consult dictionaries and encyclopedias for topics they know nothing about, or they ignore these valuable sources altogether. You'll learn several good reasons to start every research project with these sources.

- **Include law review articles:** Almost every topic you can imagine has been researched before. You can avoid reinventing the wheel by including law review articles in your research process.

- **Explore practice books, hornbooks, restatements, and other explanatory material:** These sources generally go into great depth, clearly and concisely explaining every element of the topics they cover.

- **Research legal and other news:** Legal newspapers, periodicals, and other news sources are valuable research tools.

ON THE WEB

- http://www.paralegal.delmar.cengage.com
- Annotated links leading you to:
  - Web resources for each category listed as a chapter objective
  - Exercises for additional help

INTRODUCTION

secondary sources
sources of legal information designed to give you background information and lead you to primary law.

Law librarians have a valuable research secret: Start with **secondary sources**. As most legal professionals agree, starting your research with secondary sources serves several functions.

- **You can focus on the right keywords.** Beginning your research with a secondary source like a legal encyclopedia, a legal dictionary, or words and phrases gives you a firm idea of relevant topics and leads you to appropriate legal keywords. Often, you might choose words that are not those used in cases and statutes. Starting with secondary sources helps to point you in the right direction.

law review article
article from a legal journal. Law reviews are generally based on detailed research and often focus on specialized topics. They help the researcher to find in-depth research on detailed topics.

- **You can avoid reinventing the wheel.** Hundreds of **law review articles**, **ALRs** (American Law Reports), and other sources of legal writing contain information based on in-depth research on a number of subjects. Most likely, the issue you are researching has been researched before. When you find an article on point, it generally includes an overview of the topic followed by a careful analysis of the intricacies of one portion of the subject. Hundreds of relevant cases, statutes, and additional secondary sources support this analysis, bringing you closer to your research goals.

ALR (American Law Reports)
a secondary source of legal information that has case-specific information.

- **You can deepen your perspective.** Sometimes you begin your research with a good understanding of the topic. You have an idea of where you want to go and how to focus your research appropriately. This is great, but it is possible that in narrowing your search at the outset, you eliminate other important areas to research. Reading secondary sources on your research topic helps you see the true depth of the topic and makes your end result more useful to the attorney and the client.

In addition to providing background information on a topic, another main purpose of secondary sources is to lead the researcher to primary sources. Back in the "old days" (mid-1990s) when most research was done by book, a researcher was almost forced to use secondary sources because finding the primary sources without them was so much harder. Now that electronic legal research tools are available, that heavy reliance on secondary sources to lead you to primary sources is, unfortunately, dwindling. It is simple to do a keyword search of the texts of statutes and cases and to stumble around in that fashion until you find something. However, the ease of finding primary sources online takes away none of the great reasons listed previously for beginning your research with secondary sources. The use of secondary sources is a sound strategy that professionals use and is one you should adopt as well.

Many students who run into trouble researching start their research in the wrong place. When asked where they began, they usually respond by naming the cases or statutes that they are trying, in vain, to search for. When asked why they started there, they usually have no answer. When you run into a block in your research, ask yourself where you began and why you started there. If you have no good answer, return to the Five Questions (Chapter 2) and use them to refocus. If all else fails, do not be afraid to ask an instructor or librarian for help.

Now you know all the benefits of using secondary sources. The next sections look at their electronic availability.

DICTIONARIES AND ENCYCLOPEDIAS

Legal dictionaries and **legal encyclopedias** are great places to start because both help you to focus your keywords and both help to lay a foundation for later research. Many are readily available online.

Westlaw Dictionaries and Encyclopedias

Westlaw makes some major secondary sources available on its databases. *Black's Law Dictionary* (abbreviated in Westlaw as DI)[1] and the legal encyclopedia *American Jurisprudence* (AMJUR) are great places to start.

Lexis Dictionaries and Encyclopedias

Lexis also offers some major secondary sources in its collection of secondary legal sources. *Ballentine's Law Dictionary* and the legal encyclopedia *American Jurisprudence (AmJur)* or *American Law Reports (ALR)* are great places to start.

Loislaw

Loislaw does not have a legal dictionary or legal encyclopedia as part of its database collection.

Casemaker

Casemaker's collections of secondary sources vary by state, but they currently do not include a legal dictionary or legal encyclopedia.

legal dictionary
resource for word definitions. Specific legal dictionaries are an excellent starting point for research.

legal encyclopedia
secondary source with brief explanations of legal terms and concepts, often accompanied by references to relevant cases.

The Internet's Dictionaries and Encyclopedias

Some may say that the Internet is itself a secondary source. Web pages frequently give you background information and lead you to primary sources. So you can use your basic Internet search skills to find secondary information on the Internet. Give yourself an edge by starting your search in a legal directory like FindLaw (**http://www.findlaw.com/ 15reference**) or Cornell's Wex directory (**http://www.law.cornell. edu/wex**). Directories like FindLaw and Wex make it easy to identify and browse through various categories of secondary sources. In addition, you can go to a legal directory, and find a reference section that lists a variety of legal dictionaries available on the Web.

Wikipedia (**http://www.en.wikipedia.org**) is also a popular choice. This resource is compiled by many people including legal experts. Wikipedia's Legal Portal (**http://en.wikipedia.org/**; Search for "Law Portal") is browsable and searchable, making it easy to find information. Most entries are also well documented, with links to additional resources at the end of the entry. Wikipedia is a controversial tool amongst several researchers because anyone can contribute, not just experts. You would be wise to double-check the information you find on Wikipedia to confirm that other sources agree. As a secondary source, and a controversial one at that, you should not to cite to Wikipedia. Indeed, Wikipedia itself advises against citing to it—**http://en. wikipedia.org/** (Search for "Citing Wikipedia"). However, it can be a very good starting point to lead you to secondary and primary source of law on the Internet.

Guided Exercise

As mentioned, you can use the Internet as one giant secondary source. Suppose you need to find out whether the statute of limitations has run on a particular case. You decide to start at the beginning—with the definition of the statute of limitations.

1. **Go to a legal dictionary online.** FindLaw's legal dictionary (**http://dictionary.lp.findlaw.com**) is a good one. The search box is in the center of the screen.

2. **Enter the search term in the search box.** Does it work to just enter "statute of limitations" without quotation marks? Do you need to do a formal phrase search? Read the entire definition. Does it make sense to you? Even if you know what a statute of limitations is, you might find the FindLaw's definition a little complicated.

(continued)

3. **Try to find a simpler definition.** Nolo.com (**http://www.nolo.com**) is a useful legal encyclopedia. Although it is designed for lay people, it is a great addition to your set of Web sites that you regularly refer to in your research, your toolbox of favorites. Knowing which specific sites to visit for additional information saves you a lot of time.

To get the definition, type your term in the search box and use the dropdown menu below the search box to select "search glossary" and target your search. The Nolo Web site provides additional clarification on the statute of limitations. Its plain language definition might not be the wording you would use in a legal document. However, it might be very helpful in constructing a more effective search. The drawback of sites like Nolo is that they cover only basic issues of interest to the lay person.

Exercise 8-1

Answer the following questions by using an electronic legal dictionary or encyclopedia. You can use Lexis, Westlaw, or the Internet. Support your answers by citing your sources.

1. What is *proximate cause* as it relates to the tort of negligence?
2. When does a party to a contract have to *cover*?
3. What elements are necessary to establish joint tenancy?
4. What is an example of *res ipsa loquitor*?
5. What is a *corporate veil*?
6. What is the basis of *in rem* jurisdiction?

LAW REVIEW ARTICLES

You can take advantage of others' research by searching for and reading law review articles.

Law Review Articles on Westlaw

Hundreds of legal periodicals are available in Westlaw's Law Reviews, Bar Journals, and Legal Periodicals database, from the *American Bar Association Journal* (ABAJ) to the *Yale Law and Policy Review* (YLLPR). You are probably familiar with law reviews, but you may be less familiar with **bar journals**. Bar journals differ from law reviews in one basic way: bar journals are geared toward practicing attorneys who deal with the everyday problems of running or working in a law office. Because of that, fewer bar journal articles discuss theoretical and academic approaches to the law. Rather, the articles focus on practical application of the law. You can also find very current practice topics in bar journal articles.

bar journal
legal periodical aimed at the practicing attorney.

Westlaw gives you three ways to find specific articles on your topic. First, if you have a citation, you can use the Find this Document By Citation search box to find your article. This is, as always, the easiest way to find a document. You can also search generally, using keywords to search the combined law review and bar journal database (JLR) or to perform a broader search of Major Secondary Publications (MAJSECPUBS). In the Law Review, Bar Journals, and Legal Periodicals database, you can also find *American Law Reports* (ALR), *Corpus Juris Secundum* (CJS) Restatements, and other legal texts.

The third way to search law review articles by using Westlaw is through some sort of topic grouping. You can search the law reviews of your state. (Use the two-letter state abbreviation plus JLR, for example, CA-JLR or WY-JLR.) Or, you can do a topic search. Westlaw lets you search by practice area in the Topical Materials by Area of Practice database. Just click on the Topical Practice Areas link from the All Databases page. From there, you can find combined legal periodicals under topics like Education (ED-TP), Maritime Law (MRT-TP), or Taxation (TX-TP).

If you have no ideas about the topic, try using dictionaries or encyclopedia to find some relevant information. Narrowing your search to a topic search rather than searching the broader combined law review databases generally yields more targeted results.

Law Review Articles on Lexis

Lexis has more than 200 law reviews available in its Law Reviews & Journals source. Bar journals differ from law reviews in one basic way. Bar journals' audience is practicing attorneys who are involved daily in the problems of running or working in a law office. Therefore, only a minority of articles deal with the theoretical and academic aspects of law. The majority discuss its practical application. Most bar journal articles also focus on very current practice topics. You can access the bar journals by using the Law Reviews & Journals source or using the Legal News source.

In Lexis, you can look up law review articles by citation or you can search generally, using keywords to search the US Law Reviews and Journals combined. Lexis also has law reviews grouped by topic. To access it, click on US Law Reviews and Journals > Law Review Articles by Area of Law. There is a wide variety of topics including Corporate Law, Family Law, Intellectual Property Law, and Tax Law. You will generally get better results by narrowing your search to a topic database rather than searching the combined law review sources.

Lexis also groups law review articles by state. You can access this by clicking on US Law Reviews and Journals > Law Reviews by Jurisdiction.

Loislaw

Loislaw does not have law review articles in its database collection.

A Note on Citations

As a general rule, you do not cite secondary sources in formal legal documents like court pleadings. Citing secondary sources is perfectly fine in informal legal memoranda and other informal documents. Remember that, in addition to helping you find background information, secondary sources' purpose is to lead you to primary sources of law. In formal legal documents, cite the primary sources that the secondary sources lead you to, rather than the secondary sources themselves. Be sure to fully read any documents that you cite. Do not rely on the analysis of your secondary source, as it may not fully match the facts of your case.

Law Review Articles on the Internet

There is good news and bad news regarding law reviews on the Internet. The good news is that each day, more and more law reviews and bar journals are available on the Internet. The bad news is that, unless you know the specific law review or journal that you are looking for, these sources can be hard to find.

If you know the specific law review or bar journal, you can go directly to its Web site. For example, you might want to find an article in the *Cardozo Law Review*. Do a phrase search in your favorite search engine to get its address (**http://www.cardozolawreview.com**). Alternatively, you can visit a Web page that lists a variety of law journals and browse until you find what you want. The Hiros Gamos Journals page (**http://www.hg.org/journals.html**) is a great resource. It contains a comprehensive, alphabetical listing or law review articles available on the Internet. Unfortunately, not all have the full text available to non-subscribers. Some only have abstracts or tables of contents. Thus, one huge drawback of journals on the Internet is inconvenience. Using Westlaw or Lexis, you can do a keyword search through hundreds of legal journals at the same time. Using the Internet, you must search the journals one at a time. If you were to do a general search, using a tool like Google, it would be difficult to restrict the search to law review resources, although you might luck out and find some law review resources in a broader search.

Now that you know the meaning of the terms in Exercise 8-1, find law review articles that describes each in more detail. Again, you can use Lexis, Westlaw, or the Internet. Try using a combination of resources so that you can further develop your skills. Support your answers by citing your sources. Note the subtle ways in which your queries change when you look for the same information in different places.

1. What is *proximate cause* as it relates to the tort of negligence?
2. When does a party to a contract have to *cover*?
3. What elements are necessary to establish joint tenancy?
4. What is an example of *res ipsa loquito*?
5. What is a *corporate veil*?
6. What is the basis of *in rem* jurisdiction?

PRACTICE BOOKS, HORNBOOKS, RESTATEMENTS, AND OTHER EXPLANATORY MATERIAL

These sources provide very detailed information in a clear, concise manner.

Explanatory Sources on Westlaw

Westlaw libraries have a great selection of valuable secondary sources. You can access the information in a few ways. If you know that a specific secondary source exists, you can use the Find a Database Wizard to find the publication and then do a keyword search of that source only.

Instructions: Use the Find a Database Wizard to find a specific publication by following these steps:

1. From the Westlaw main search page, click on the Find a Database Wizard.
2. What are you trying to find? Select Publication or Other Source.
3. Next, choose your geographic location.
4. Next, type in the name of the specific publication you are looking for.
5. Finally, choose a database to search, either limited to the specific publication or expanded to include other publications as well.

If you do not have the name of a specific publication, you can use some similar steps to get a list of categories and names of individual secondary sources to search.

Instructions: Use the Find a Database Wizard to find topical databases by following these steps:

1. From the Westlaw main search page, click on the Find a Database Wizard.
2. What are you trying to find? Select Practice or Research Area Materials.
3. Next, choose your geographic location.
4. Next, type in the topic you are looking for.
5. Finally, choose a database to search, either limited to the specific publication or expanded to include other publications as well.

You can search the sources that you find independently or in a combined search of tort-related periodicals, texts, and journals (TRT-TP).

A third alternative is to do a global search of all texts and periodicals combined (TP-ALL), using a selection of keywords. This is a good choice if you are not entirely sure of the topic or if you would like to broaden your research horizon.

Explanatory Sources on Lexis

Lexis has a variety of **practice books**, **hornbooks**, and **restatements**. There are a few ways to access that information. If you know that a specific secondary source exists, you can search for and to find the publication by using Lexis' Find a Source tab and then search only that source for keywords.

If you do not know a specific publication's name, you can browse the Area of Law Treatises under Secondary Legal. That leads you to the names of categories or individual secondary sources to search. Suppose you want information on contracts. If you browse through the list, you will run across *Farnsworth on Contracts*.

practice book
legal reference aimed at the practicing attorney. Often in a three-ring binder, the practice book is meant to be a current reference on everything relevant to its specific subject area.

hornbook
textbook-like, in-depth, and with detailed exploration of a broad legal topic like torts or contracts.

restatement
textbook-like exploration of a single legal subject for which most law is developed in the courts.

Read What You Cite

When you find a secondary source with a wealth of cases on point, relying on the analysis that you find there is tempting. It is also tempting to include that analysis in your research results. After all, the authors are the experts, and you do not want to reinvent the wheel. You must avoid the temptation to adopt the professional's analysis as your own. You need to read the key primary sources so that you can draw your own conclusions as they relate to your unique set of facts. You should read every case or statute that you cite in your final document. And don't forget to Shepardize!

Another alternative is to globally search a combination of secondary sources by using a selection of keywords. This approach is good if you are not entirely sure of the topic or if you want to broaden your research.

Explanatory Sources on Loislaw

Loislaw has a selection of state continuing legal education (CLE) materials. CLE materials are aimed at the practicing attorney and, like the practice book, present useful information about the law as it is practiced in the field. Although Loislaw's CLE materials are not available for every state, you may find looking at another state's materials useful in developing your research.

Explanatory Sources on Casemaker

Casemaker's materials vary by state. Be sure to check your state's library to see if any explanatory materials are available.

Explanatory Sources on the Internet

The Internet is also a disappointing option for finding hornbooks and practice books online. This is because these books tend to be privately published and thus are not freely available on the Internet. You may find that the information is available on the Internet for a small fee, but if you have access Westlaw or Lexis, they are a better bet.

LEGAL AND OTHER NEWS

You will find a wide variety of legal newspapers, periodicals, and other news sources available online. These are valuable resources for research.

News Sources on Westlaw

Westlaw's selection of legal news sources is bound to help you find the information you need. You can search the Combined News Databases in general (ALLNEWS) or state-by-state (using the two-letter state abbreviation plus NEWS, for example, HI-NEWS or FL-NEWS). Use the Business and News tab to access a variety of links leading to news resources. There, you can find not only legal, business and international news, but general interest magazines, newsletters, and television transcripts of programs like *60 Minutes* (60MIN) are also available. Collections include both national and international holdings. This variety of options in categorizing legal news makes it easy for you to effectively narrow the focus of your search.

News Sources on Lexis

Lexis organizes legal news by topic, jurisdiction, jury verdicts, and other. Using the other link you can search the most recent news made in the last 90 days as well as current news from the past two years. Legal newsletters on specific areas of law are also available, including "Entertainment Law," "Insurance Law," and "School Law." Collections include both national and international holdings. This variety of options in categorizing legal news makes it easy for you to effectively narrow the focus of your search.

News Sources on Loislaw, Casemaker, and the Internet

Though Loislaw and Casemaker do not carry much legal news, several Web sites provide excellent legal news and analysis. Many major news outlets, like the *CNN* (**http://www.CNN.com**), have special sections on legal news (**http://www.cnn.com/law/**). General sources like Google News (**http://news.google.com**) will send the news to you. You can use Google Alerts to run a specific news search for you and send you the results by e-mail on a regular basis. Indeed, many news providers, including Westlaw and Lexis, provide legal news by e-mail. This is an excellent and relatively painless way to stay on top of the subjects most important to you or your client.

SUMMARY

Secondary sources have been and will continue to be an excellent way to begin legal research. They lead you to key cases; they give you expert, in-depth analysis; and they help you to focus your search. Secondary sources also assist you by adding depth and perspective, especially when you do not know the subject matter very well. Secondary sources are simple to access and provide a wealth of information. Do not neglect this most important step of legal research.

Chapter Review Exercises

Find answers to the following questions by using secondary sources. Note the secondary sources in which you find your answers. The words in italics give you great terms to use to start your search.

1. Josie worked as a maid for Happy Housecleaners. She enjoyed her job, especially because she got to view beautiful things every day in the houses she visited. However, the more beautiful things that Josie saw, the more she wanted them for herself. One day, while cleaning the home of the wealthy Mrs. Miser, Josie saw a lovely figurine of a woman with her cat. She just had to have it. The small figurine was on a shelf with dozens of other figurines. Josie doubted Mrs. Miser would miss it. She slipped the figurine into her pocket and took it home, where she gave it a place of honor on her mantle.

   Two days later, the police came for Josie and charged her with theft. Mrs. Miser also wanted to sue Happy Housecleaners for damages under the theory of *respondeat superior*, because Josie was their employee. Can Mrs. Miser sue Happy Housecleaners under this theory?

2. The elderly yet spry Magdelina Esperanza Guapa lived in a small house that she had inherited as a *life estate* from her mother. After Magdelina's death, the house was to go to her niece Estrella. Magdelina did not like Estrella, because the girl tended to be flighty and got engaged to a different young man every few months. So Magdelina sold the small house to her gardener, Jorge, for a bargain price, hoping that Estrella would never get the house. Magdelina moved to a retirement condominium where she had an active social life until she died three years later.

   Two weeks after Magdelina's funeral, Estrella went to the little house and demanded that Jorge surrender it to her. Does Jorge have any rights here, or does he have to surrender the house to Estrella?

3. Skipper was selling her boat, the *Malibu*, for $50,000. Kev saw the boat and really wanted to buy it, but he had to ask his wife first. Kev offered Skipper $200 to hold the offer open to him for two days. Skipper agreed to the *firm offer* proposal. The next day, another buyer came along and offered $55,000. Skipper knew this was much more than Kev could offer, so she accepted and sold the boat to the other buyer.

   Kev came back two days later with his wife's permission. He was devastated when Skipper gave him the $200 back, saying she had already sold the boat. Kev wonders whether he has any recourse against Skipper for breaching their agreement. Does he?

Worksheet

Secondary Source Research Toolbox

Use this chart to comment on the Web sites listed and to include information on your favorites.

Web site: Westlaw (**http://www.westlaw.com**)

Favorite Features:

Comments:

Web site: Lexis (**http://www.lexis.com**)

Favorite Features:

Comments:

Web site: Loislaw (**http://www.loislaw.com**)

Favorite Features:

Comments:

Web site: Casemaker *(available from the Web site of your state bar association)*

Favorite Features:

Comments:

Web site: FindLaw (**http://www.findlaw.com**)

Favorite Features:

Comments:

Web site: Cornell's Wex Directory (**http://www.law.cornell.edu/wex/**)

Favorite Features:

Comments:

Web site: Wikipedia (**http://www.en.wikipedia.org**)

Favorite Features:

Comments:

Web site: Nolo (http://www.nolo.com)

Favorite Features:

Comments:

Web site: Cardozo Law Review (**http://www.cardozolawreview.com**)

Favorite Features:

Comments:

Web site: Hiros Gamos (**http://www.hg.org/journals.html**)

Favorite Features:

Comments:

Web site: CNN (**http://www.cnn.com**)

Favorite Features:

Comments:

Web site: *Google News* (http://news.google.com)

Favorite Features:

Comments:

Web site:

Favorite Features:

Comments:

Web site:

Favorite Features:

Comments:

Web site:

Favorite Features:

Comments:

Web site:

Favorite Features:

Comments:

Web site:

Favorite Features:

Comments:

Worksheet

New Database Worksheet

Use this worksheet to record the relevant search information you discover when you explore new databases.

Database:

Boolean search:

Proximity search:

Phrase search:

Stemming:

Wildcard:

Researcher's Guide to the U.S. Government

THE THREE BRANCHES OF GOVERNMENT

The U.S. federal government is divided into three branches: the executive branch, the legislative branch, and the judicial branch. The executive branch includes the president, the Cabinet and all of the executive agencies. The legislative branch includes the Senate and the House of Representatives. The judicial branch includes all of the federal courts including the U.S. Supreme Court, the U.S. Circuit Courts, and the U.S. District Courts. Each of these branches has some lawmaking power, and understanding the types of laws that each branch creates is essential to effective research.

   This appendix focuses on the federal government but may also be applicable to state governments. Each state government also has three branches. The executive branch includes the governor and the state agencies; the legislative branch generally has a house of representatives and a senate; and the judicial branch has the state courts. So you can use the information in this guide to assist you in finding state resources as well.

APPENDIX A

THE LEGISLATIVE BRANCH

The legislative branch is the primary lawmaking branch. It creates statutes that, at the federal level, are found in the United States Code (USC).

THE EXECUTIVE BRANCH

The executive branch makes law primarily through its administrative agencies. After the legislative branch creates statutory law, the administrative agencies create regulations to further develop and explain the statutory law. At the federal level, statutes can be found in the Code of Federal Regulations (CFR).

THE JUDICIAL BRANCH

The judicial branch is tasked primarily with interpreting the law. However, through its interpretations of law, it creates law as well. The case law the judicial branch creates is also known as common law. At the federal level, case law can be found in different places depending on the level of court. The federal district courts report cases in the Federal Supplement (F. Supp.); appellate courts report cases in the Federal Reporter (F.). The U.S. Supreme Court reports in three places: the United States Supreme Court Reports (US), the Supreme Court Reporter (S. Ct.), and the Lawyers Edition of the Supreme Court Reports (L. Ed.).

Legislative History

OVERVIEW OF LEGISLATIVE HISTORY

Your legal research text should have a section on legislative history and the tools available to perform it. Here is a quick review to help you understand the tools available to simplify your research. Keep in mind that the tools available for doing federal legislative history are likely to differ from those available for state legislative history.

FEDERAL LEGISLATIVE HISTORY

The best way to understand the process of researching legislative history is to understand the legislative process.

First, the proposed bill is introduced in either the Senate or the House of Representatives. At this point, the bill is numbered and sent to a congressional committee for review. It may be amended, rewritten altogether, or not acted on at all. If the bill is not acted on at all, then the bill "dies in committee."

You can look at the *Congressional Index* for information on active bills, including bills in committee. Published every week while Congress is in session, it chronologically lists all bills being considered and includes basic information about their status. For information on bills in committee, you may also turn to the *United States Code, Congressional and Administrative News (USCCAN)*. This valuable resource contains the full text of selected committee reports and useful citations to related documents in the *Congressional Record*.

A committee may hold hearings on the proposed bill. The *Congressional Information Service's (CIS) Index and Abstract* contains information on congressional hearings. The index includes the publications of more than 300 congressional committees.

bill tracking
following the progress of legislation as it
moves from its original proposal through
committees to potential passing and signing
by the executive.

legislative history
documentation of the process that a bill went
through to become a law. Often used to
interpret the law after its passage.

After the committee acts on the bill, it reports back to the Senate or the House for debate and, potentially, a vote on the bill. The *Congressional Record* (**http://www.gpoaccess.gov/crecord/**) reports the full text of debates in both the House and the Senate. If the House votes on and passes the bill, the entire process repeats in the Senate. The reverse is also true—if the Senate votes on and passes the bill, the entire process repeats itself in the house.

Bills passed by both the House and the Senate make it to the president's desk. The president can either sign or veto the bill. The *Weekly Compilation of Presidential Documents* (**http://www.gpoaccess.gov/wcomp/**) includes veto and signing messages.

By looking at these publications, a researcher can do two things. First, you can follow an active bill as it goes through the process of becoming law. This is known as **bill tracking**. Second, you can look at the same process from a historical perspective and determine—from debates, reports, and the like—what the drafters meant to accomplish when they wrote the law. This is **legislative history**.

STATE LEGISLATIVE HISTORY

Each of the 50 states has a law-making process similar to that of the federal government. Of course, each state has different legislative structures and presents relevant information in different publications. The Online Companion contains links that explain how to do legislative history in nearly every state in the Union. The Web sites for your state law library and state archives are also excellent resources to help you to investigate state legislative history.

LEGISLATIVE HISTORY RESOURCES

To research and learn about legislative history, you can refer to the many electronic sources described in this text. They include Westlaw and Lexis, as well as a variety of federal and state-specific resources on the Internet.

LEGISLATIVE HISTORY ON WESTLAW

Westlaw's Federal Statutes, Legislative History, and Bill Tracking database lets you access federal legislative history easily. Federal resources include the *Congressional Record* (CR), *Congressional Testimony* (CONGTMY or USTESTIMONY), and *Congressional Quarterly's Washington Alert* for bill tracking (CQ-BILLTRK) and its full text of bills (CQ-BILLTXT). This database also has a compilation of legislative histories from Arnold & Porter. In addition, you can find legislative histories under its individual topic areas. For example, in the Finance and Banking database, you can find Arnold & Porter's *Riegle History of the Community Development and Regulatory Improvement Act of 1994* (RIEGLE94-LH).

For state legislative history and bill tracking, Westlaw facilitates bill tracking (e.g., NY-BILLTRK) and viewing the full text of bills (e.g., NY-BILLTXT) for all 50 states. For researching older legislation, Westlaw's Historical Legislative Service covers each state and laws dating back to the early 1990s. You can find these resources in the Statute and Court Rules directory for each state.

This is just a sample of materials available for researching legislative history on Westlaw. To see all that is available, view the Westlaw Directory for each state and the federal government.

LEGISLATIVE HISTORY ON LEXIS

The Legislation Library on Lexis includes information about researching both state and federal legislation. You'll find it under Legislation and Politics – US & UK on the Look for a Source section of Lexis. Federal resources for the United States include the *Congressional Record*, full text of bills, Senate and House debates, and the *Daily Digest*. Lexis has also compiled and organized legislative histories by topic (e.g., the compiled bankruptcy legislative histories) and by specific act (e.g., the legislative history of the Toxic Substances Control Act). To find the compiled legislative histories, click on Legislation and Politics – US & UK > US Congress > Legislative Histories. The Legislation Library also includes news sources, Bureau of National Affairs (BNA) daily reports on a variety of topics, and a host of other resources.

For state legislative history and bill tracking, Lexis provides the full text of current and past bills for all 50 states. To access these resources, click on Legislation and Politics – US & UK > US States. Lexis also has current bill-tracking information and bill-tracking archives that contain material dating back to 1990.

This is just a sample of the materials available for researching legislative history on Lexis. Accessing a list of the full collection of materials in the Legislation Library is easy—just click on Legislation and Politics—US & UK and follow the links from there. On Lexis.com, click Legislation and Politics, then click U.S. Congress.

LEGISLATIVE HISTORY ON LOISLAW

Focused on state materials, Loislaw currently has no resources for researching federal or state legislative history or tracking bills.

LEGISLATIVE HISTORY ON THE INTERNET

The Internet is an excellent resource for bill tracking, checking recent legislative history, and finding compiled legislative histories of popular topics. Thomas (**http://thomas.loc.gov/**) is the major resource for current congressional information. Published by the Library of Congress, Thomas divides the information from the U. S. Code Congressional & Administrative News USSCAN into several sections, including Bills & Resolutions, Congressional Record, and Committee Reports. The Bills and Resolutions section includes bill summaries and a public law index that dates back to 1973. Full texts of bills are available dating back to 1989. The *Congressional Record* has the full text dating back to 1989, and the *Congressional Index* dates back to 1994. The Committee Reports section has committee reports dating back to the 104th Congress (1995–1996), as well as links to committee Web pages. The Current Activities section tracks bills currently on the House floor. Overall, this is an excellent site.

Exhibit B–1 Thomas Web site.

You can also go directly to the source. Both the House (**http://www. house.gov**) and the Senate (**http://www.senate.gov**) have quick links from their main pages to an index of committees. A visit to the Web page of the Senate Banking, Housing, and Urban Affairs Committee (**http:// banking.senate.gov/**) is illustrative. There, the researcher can find hearing information, the full text of committee reports, and links to other information relevant to committee activities.

Another way to find information about legislation is by visiting the Web sites of interested parties. For example, the American Civil Liberties Union (**http://www.aclu.org**) has an in-depth Web site that includes information on all issues of interest to the ACLU. The ACLU's main page has an issues index that includes everything from criminal justice to workplace rights. Under each topic are documents and news briefs on breaking issues, as well as historical documents on the topic.

The American Association of Retired Persons (**http://www.aarp.org**) is another example of an interest group that provides easy access to information on topics important to its members. From its main page, visitors can click on the Issues and Elections link to review issues regarding health, housing, and economic security. This site also includes summaries of AARP testimony to Congress.

For information on state resources, try the Web sites of the state law library or local law school libraries. They frequently have information on the process of state legislative history and links to any available on-line resources. You could also check out the local branches of interest groups like the ones mentioned previously.

LEGISLATIVE HISTORY SEARCH STRATEGY

One of the toughest parts of researching legislative history is figuring out where to start. The Legislative History Search Strategy we present here should eliminate that problem by guiding you through the early steps of legislative history research.

STEP 1: DETERMINE WHY YOU ARE DOING THE RESEARCH

Before you begin any research, you should clearly understand why you are doing the research. That might mean forming an issue question or figuring out the meaning of a word. Why are you doing this legislative history? Sometimes you just need a general history of a bill, with no particular issue. More often than not, however, you hope the history clarifies some issue or explains some term. With a clear idea of the issue or your reason for researching legislative history, you can make an intelligent decision about how to proceed. That may mean that you do not need to follow all the steps in this process, or it may mean that you need to take several more steps to find your answer.

STEP 2: GET A COPY OF THE STATUTE

Having an actual copy of the statute helps you determine several things, including the following:

- What is the bill number?
- What year did the bill pass?
- Has the law been amended? When?

The information that you need is generally at the end of a statute. Here is an example of a federal statute, the Public Hearings section of the Coastal Zone Management Act.

16 USCS § 1457 (2000)
§ 1457. Public hearings

All public hearings required under this title must be announced at least thirty days prior to the hearing date. At the time of the announcement, all agency materials pertinent to the hearings, including documents, studies, and other data, must be made available to the public for review and study. As similar materials are subsequently developed, they shall be made available to the public as they become available to the agency.

HISTORY: (June 17, 1966, P.L. 89-454, Title III, § 311 [308], as added Oct. 27, 1972, P.L. 92-583, 86 Stat. 1287; July 26, 1976, P.L. 94-370, § 7, 90 Stat. 1019.)

The history section at the end of a statute has a plethora of useful information. First, the law in our example was proposed as Public Law (P.L.) 89-454 and signed into law on June 17, 1966. This section of the Act was amended in October of 1972 and again in 1976, as Public Law 94-370. With this information, you can easily use the resources mentioned. Keep in mind that, during the process of becoming a law, the bill is not yet codified—in other words, it has not been placed in the United States Code with a handy number like 16 USC 1457. Rather, during the consideration stage, laws are referred to by their public law number. As you can see, researching legislative history would be impossible without having the public law number available.

The information at the end of a statute also arms you with the information needed to do some comparative research. Is your research issue current, or did the matter arise some time ago? Did the law read differently at that time? Does the current or the former law apply to your issue? Are the changes in the law's language relevant to your issue? The answers to those questions, if relevant to your issue, may lead you to important information.

Historical Research

When doing research electronically, you are generally guaranteed the most up-to-date version of the law. That is wonderful—if the most current version of the law is what you want. Often, when researching legislative history, you are interested in reading older versions of the law. To find out if there are old versions, look to the current version of the law for the original passage date and the dates of any amendments.

You can find old versions of the law in hard copy in the libraries of larger law schools or the law library associated with your state capitol. Both Westlaw and Lexis have selected archive versions of statutes at both the state and federal level.

Generally the same type of information follows state statutes as follows federal statutes. If you are uncertain what the abbreviations at the end mean, now may be a good time to actually open a book (abbreviations are always defined in the first few pages) or pick up the phone and call a local law librarian. Sometimes electronic researchers feel boxed in by their computers and forget that other resources are available. Remember that the telephone is also a great research tool. You generally have a variety of resources available to you. The skillful researcher knows how and when to use them all.

STEP 3: DOES A LEGISLATIVE HISTORY ALREADY EXIST FOR THIS BILL?

Often the information in compiled legislative histories is all you need to answer your question. You could try a quick Web search, using your bill name and the phrase *legislative history*. Alternatively, you could specifically check various sources. For federal law, check *USCCAN, Congressional Information Services,* and the *Congressional Record.* They often have citations to existing legislative histories. Also, the annotated version of a statute may have information about existing histories or detailed law review articles that include a historical perspective. Both Westlaw and Lexis have sections with existing legislative histories that you can easily search. Often Westlaw and Lexis include direct links to research resources, including law review articles and existing legislative histories, at the bottom of a bill. Existing legislative histories can save you a great deal of work. People who are experts in their respective fields created most of the compiled legislative histories. Thus, a compiled legislative history can give you a more global perspective, which may be hard to obtain if you are not already intimately familiar with the subject matter that the statute addresses.

STEP 4: WHAT OTHER SPECIFIC INFORMATION DO I NEED?

Steps 1 through 4 should give you a general legislative history and answer many of your questions about the legislation. If you need to answer a more specific question, however, those steps may not be enough, especially if you cannot find an existing legislative history. If that is the case, you may need to begin to compile your own legislative history, using the materials noted here. Refer to your legal research text for more information on compiling legislative histories.

Regulatory Guidance and Rule Tracking

INTRODUCTION

Regulatory guidance is the regulatory version of legislative history. Regulatory interpretation or guidance is information from an agency about how it intends to interpret its law. That "straight-from-the-horse's mouth" information can be invaluable for the regulated community because it greatly reduces the guesswork of trying to figure out what regulations really mean. Although a regulation's purpose is to clarify statutes written by Congress or the state legislature, sometimes the clarification needs clarifying. That's where guidance comes in.

REVIEW OF THE RULE-MAKING PROCESS

Before a bill becomes a law, several steps must be completed. The same is true before a regulation becomes a final rule. (The words *rule* and *regulation* are used interchangeably.)

1. **The agency proposes the rule.** Sometimes, the agency creates a draft rule independently; other times, the agency invites interested parties to participate in drafting the proposed rule.
2. **The agency publishes the proposed rule for comment.** Federal rules are published in the *Federal Register*, a daily publication available from the Government Printing Office **(http://www.gpoaccess.gov)**. Many states also publish public information in registers.
3. **The agency accepts public comment.** During the comment period, the comments can be presented in writing or in person at a public meeting.
4. **Agencies must respond to public comments.** If the response results in major changes to the proposed rule, then the agency must re-propose the rule. However, if changes are minor or if none are made, the agency creates the final rule.

5. **The agency publishes the final rule, generally with some comments.** This occurs after all comment periods are over to let parties know when the rule takes effect and who is subject to the new rule.
6. **The rule is codified in the Code of Federal Regulations or in the state regulatory code.**

EXPLANATION OF REGULATORY GUIDANCE

Regulatory guidance consists mainly of comments that accompany the rules at various stages of publication. Some agencies also publish separate guidance or policy documents specifically for the purpose of clarifying a confusing rule or explaining the rule's enforcement. Another source of regulatory guidance is agency correspondence to members of the regulated community who formally request regulatory interpretation. These combined sources can go a long way toward explaining a regulation with an unclear meaning. As mentioned earlier, finding regulatory guidance is relatively simple compared to finding legislative history. Follow the steps in Chapter 6, and you should be on your way.

RULE TRACKING

The rule-making process looks at agency thought process and requirements. By contrast, rule tracking focuses on following the actual rule through the rule-making process. Fortunately, doing so is not too difficult, because you generally use the same sources that you used for regulatory guidance. To start, look to the *Federal Register*, or your state version of it, for the publication of proposed rules.

An alternative to tracking the rule yourself is to ask the agency to do the work for you. Most agencies maintain lists of interested parties on a variety of issues. If you are interested in an issue, contact the relevant agency and let them know. The agency will then send you notices regarding upcoming rules, the progress of proposed rules, and public meetings regarding those rules.

Research databases are also useful tools in tracking regulations. Both Westlaw (US-REGTRK) and Lexis provide specialized directories for tracking regulations. In Lexis, you can access the RegAlert by looking under the Legislation & Politics – US & UK link. You can also track state regulations by accessing the administrative law section of each individual state. At this time, Loislaw does not include specialized tools for regulation tracking.

On the Internet, the relevant agency Web site is again your best bet. However, if you are interested in reviewing some opinions along the way, visiting the Web sites of interested parties might also be useful. For example, in 1999 the Federal Deposit Insurance Corporation (FDIC; **http://www.fdic.gov**) proposed a set of regulations known as the Know Your Customer rules. These Regulatory Guidance rules required banks to monitor its customers with larger than normal financial transactions. The regulations aimed to reduce money laundering. Outraged privacy groups posted extensive information about the proposed rules on their Web sites. The groups hoped to get their members to submit comments on the proposed rules during the comment period. The privacy groups achieved astonishing success, causing the agency to withdraw the Know Your Customer rules before they became final. So Web sites of organizations that might be interested in the outcome of proposed regulation are another good information source during the rulemaking process. Find this information by doing a general search for the name of your regulation. Try it out by doing a phrase search on Google or your favorite search engine for "Know Your Customer" and you'll see the kind of information available, even for an older rule.

25 Tips to Improve Your Internet Research Skills

SEARCH TIPS FOR POWER USERS

1. Use the Help Section

Every major search tool has a help section. Go to the help section on your favorite search tool and read how it handles Boolean search terms including phrase searching. See whether you can limit results by date, or type of site, or type of media. When you learn how a search tool works and regularly use that knowledge, you'll find your searching is far more effective.

For comprehensive searching, try **Google (http://www.google.com)** or **All the Web (http://www.alltheweb.com)**.

APPENDIX **D**

2. Use Boolean Searching

You use it in Lexis and Westlaw, but did you know that you could use Boolean searching on the Internet as well. It varies from search tool to search tool, so be sure to refer to Tip Number 1.

Common Boolean search terms include:

- AND (+)
- NOT (−)
- OR (/)
- Phrase searching ("quotation marks" or (parentheses))

3. Understand the Invisible Web

When searching for your query, search engines look for keywords in the text of a document. As such, there are several things that search engines generally don't find. For example, you might have trouble finding images, streaming media or sound files, Adobe PDF documents, and the like.

Contents in databases also evade the detection of most search engines. This information, though on the Internet, can be hard to find. It is this information that makes up the invisible or deep Web.

To tap into the invisible Web, you can try the media specific searching on tools like Google or Yahoo! (which have specific search options for images, PDF documents, and translates pages in foreign languages). In addition, you might want to try a specialized search tool like **FindLaw** (**http://www.findlaw.com**), which allows you to search the Web for sites with legal content. If you are searching an area that you are unfamiliar with and you don't know of any specialized search tools, try the **Complete Planet** (**http://www.completeplanet.com**).

4. Learn to Use Your Browser Effectively

Whether you use Internet Explorer, Netscape, Opera or another browser, there are probably some handy shortcuts that can save you time when cruising the information superhighway.

- **Forward and Back:** The top of your browser has buttons that allow you to go back and forth through the Web pages that you have visited since logging on. If you want to go back to a site you visited several pages ago, you can get the list of the last 8 or 10 pages you visited. In Netscape, click the back button and hold it down to see the list or go to "Go" on the menu bar. In Explorer, click on the little downward arrow next to the back button to get the list.

- **Bookmarks/Favorites:** Save your favorite sites by adding them to your bookmarks. In Netscape, click on "Bookmarks" and your first choice is to "Add to Bookmarks." In Explorer, click on "Favorites" and select "Add to Favorites."

Both browsers allow you to edit your bookmarks as well. You may want to organize your favorite sites into folders. For example, you might want to have a legal research folder for the Web sites you use for legal research. In addition, while editing, you can change the name of the bookmark. Sometimes the name the Web site designer gave to a page will not help you remember it in the future. In Netscape, while in the edit page, right click on the link and select Properties. From there, you can type in a new name for the link. In Explorer, simply select "change name."

If you have a lot of bookmarks, you may want to use a bookmark management system like **Spurl** (**http://www.spurl.net**) or **Delicious** (**http://del.icio.us**).

- **Find in Page:** This is a great tool. Once you find a Web page that supposedly has the information you want, you are stuck scrolling through the whole page, trying to find what you like. Instead, you can save time by using the "Find in page" feature. Simply go to "Edit" on the menu bar and select "Find in page." You can then type in the term you are searching for. This feature is available in most Windows programs.

- **Setting Your Home Page:** You have complete control over the page that first opens in your Web browser. Choose the page you tend to go to first when you get on line. To make that your new home page, go to that page. If you are in Netscape, go to "Edit" and "Preferences." In the middle of the dialog box are the Homepage settings. Click on the "Current Page" button to set that page as your new homepage. In Explorer, go to "View" and "Internet Options." The first section has the Homepage settings. Click on the "current page" button to set that page as your new homepage.

- **History:** Your browser automatically keeps track of every page you visit for several days. You can access this information on the History page. In Netscape, go to "Communicator," "Tools" and "History." In Explorer, there is a "History" icon.

- **Text Size:** You can change the size of most text by using the text size feature. You'll find it in most browsers under the "view" menu, select "text size." Note that this does not work for text embedded in graphics.

5. Create a Research Toolbox

There are thousands of search tools on the Web. Some people use the same tool for everything, but, depending on the type of research you do, it may make more sense to use to use certain tools for certain types of searching. For example, you might want to use **Clusty** (**http://www.clusty.com**) when doing very broad-based searching, aided by its custom search folders. Once you determine the types of searching you generally do, determine your top two favorites in each category, study their help areas and let those tools be your starting point whenever researching. This will make your searching faster, less frustrating, and more effective.

SECURITY AND PRIVACY ONLINE

6. Understanding Viruses

Viruses Defined: programs that reprogram your computer to do things you don't want. Viruses have two aspects: vector and payload.

- **Vector:** how the virus propagates (files on floppy disks or email; Web sites)
- **Payload:** what the virus does other than propagate (mess up documents, delete files, attack other computers)

Defense by vector
- **Files:** Use antivirus software and keep "signatures" up to date
- **Email:** "Show extensions"; Turn off email html options
- **Web sites:** set browser to warn when sites write on your hard drive
- On/Off switch

Defense by payload
- Backup, backup, backup
- Turn off macros (and check this after any virus attack)
- Consider use of products that are not so vulnerable to attack. Not all vendors let programs reprogram your computer so easily.

7. Confirming Hoaxes

Does it sound too good, weird, or awful to be true? It probably is. Whenever you get an email warning you of a hoax, before you get all worried, take a moment to check it out. Most of the main virus protection Web sites have excellent and up-to-date information on viruses. In addition, if you go to the Web site of your virus software, it will likely have a patch for any valid viruses.
Resources include:

- **McAfee (http://www.mcafee.com)**
- **Norton (http://www.symantec.com)**
- **Snopes (http://www.snopes.com)**

8. Understand Privacy Encroachment

Privacy: Many Web sites give you the information that you want in exchange for the information that they want—your e-mail address and other personal information. Web sites then often sell this information along with your search and/or shopping preferences to other organizations who use that information to market to you more effectively.
One way you can protect yourself in this environment is to have a special e-mail address that you use for registering for things. There are dozens of free Web based e-mail programs available.

Return Address: Web sites hold on to your computer address (IP address) and can use it, together with other information, to put together a profile of you.

- **Anonomizer Service:** Gives you anonymity when you are moving around the Internet. It is not ethically required by most Bar Associations.
- Change your IP address frequently. You can set your modem to do this automatically.

9. Understand Risks of Always On Connection

If you have a DSL or Cable connection, your connection is "always on." Use a filter of some sort to prevent your computer from being used by hackers. You can use a firewall to protect yourself.

10. Limiting Information Sharing

It is generally true that you don't get anything for free. Many Web sites are able to give you free access to resources with advertising, subscriptions or selling your personal information. Read the privacy statement before giving an Web site information about you or your business. However, be aware that recently, the downturn in the tech industry has caused some sites to go back on their promises and sell the data when liquidating the business.

You may accidentally be sending information you don't intend to when sending Word documents. Word's Track Changes feature allows changes and comments to be viewed.

You can also limit exposure by using a Web-based e-mail service to use for registrations. That way, even if your information is sold, you won't have your main e-mail deluged with unwanted messages.

For more information about online privacy, try these sites:

- **Electronic Privacy Information Center (http://www.epic.org)**
- **The Privacy Site (http://www.privacy.org)**

GREAT GENERAL SEARCH TIPS

11. Don't get Stuck on One Search Tool

Sure, most experts agree that **Google (http://www.google.com)** is the best search tool out there (at the moment). But, believe it or not, studies show that the exact same search done on several different search tools can yield substantially different results. What that means is that, while you should start with your favorite search tool, branch out and try a different tool if you don't find what you are looking for. Some new ones to try include:

- **All the Web** (**http://www.alltheweb.com**) was recently voted the second best search engine by Search Engine Watch Awards. Find out what all the hype is about.
- **Hot Bot** (**http://www.hotbot.com**) has recently made a comeback in the search engine world.

12. Use Directories

By now, you should realize that all searching is not the same. Indeed, you are often better off not searching, but browsing. Directories can be great browsing starting points. Go to a directory compiled by people you trust and you'll save hours in your research. You might want to try **Librarian's Index to the Internet** (**http://www.lii.org**) and the **Open Directory Project** (**http://www.dmoz.org**).

13. News Searching

If you are doing news based research, you'll want to use a specialized tool. Try **Google News** (**http://news.google.com**) or **Yahoo News** (**http://news.yahoo.com**). For legal specific news, try **FindLaw News** (**http://news.findlaw.com**) or **CNN**'s legal section (**http://www.cnn.com/law**). News searching is tough to do with even the best search engines. These powerful, news specific search tools make it all much simpler.

14. Follow a Weblog (blog or blawg)

Weblogs are a form of online journaling that help shrink the Internet assist you in learning things you might not otherwise have known. Lawyers have jumped onto the blog bandwagon with great enthusiasm. Check out the link below for some of my favorite legal Weblogs.

- **SCOTUS Blog:** A Weblog about the daily activities of the U.S. Supreme Court (**http://www.scotusblog.com**)
- **Inter-Alia:** A legal research Weblog (**http://www.inter-alia.net**)
- **Blawg.org:** Discover your own favorites using this legal Weblog directory (**http://www.blawg.org**).
- Here is a nice article on blogging from famous blogger **Ernie the Attorney** on LLRX (**http://www.llrx.com/features/lawyerWeblogs.htm**).

15. Research Newsletters

There is an ocean of information on the Internet and it is difficult and time consuming to try to sift through it all. Fortunately, several enterprising souls have taken care of that problem for you with research newsletters. Some come daily, weekly or monthly and are full of information about general and specific research. This is an especially good way to get information about specialty practice areas.

Several of these newsletters are mentioned throughout the materials. Some good starting points for legal resources include:

- **Internet Legal Research Weekly (http://www.inter-alia.net)**
- **Research Buzz:** Put out by super searcher Tara Calishain (**http://www.researchbuzz.com**)

BEST LEGAL RESOURCES

16. LegalWA.org

LegalWA.org (http://www.legalwa.org) is a cooperative effort between WSBA, MRSC, and Washington's Code Reviser to provide the Washington legal community with free access to the law. It provides an impressive collection of Washington appellate and Supreme Court case law, statutes, regs and municipal codes.

17. FindLaw

FindLaw (http://www.findlaw.com) has long been a leader in legal research. FindLaw is a search tool that focuses on legal search. It not only connects you to Web based resources, it has a vast database of its own. Since its acquisition by Westlaw, it has moved into the portal business, with e-mail, news, chat, and more. You can also access some fee based Westlaw services as well.

18. University of Southern California–Journal Search

Finding legal journals on the Web is generally a hit or miss operation. The **University Law Review Project** has made it a little easier with its **search tool (http://www.lawreview.org)**. If your favorite journal lacks a search tool, try using Google's site search feature.

19. Hieros Gamos

If your legal research involves international law, you should try **Hieros Gamos (http://www.hg.org)**. Hieros Gamos is a great first stop, acting as a search engine and directory. If you get information in foreign languages, don't forget to try the translation tools in Alta Vista and Google. I also recommend LLRX, which frequently features articles on searching foreign law. Look under **Zimmerman's Research Guide** (**http://www.lexisnexis.com/infopro/zimmerman**) and search your country.

20. Law Library Web sites

Few people know more about legal research than law librarians. As such, you would be wise to refer to Web sites created by and for librarians. Here are a few of my favorites.

University of Washington Gallagher Law Library's Web page is a great source of local and national law on the Web. Check out their site for what is new in primary sources and other kinds of law (**http://lib.law.washington.edu/research/research.html**). You should also try the Web site of the **Washington State Law Library** (**http://www.courts.wa.gov**). Other law school and state law libraries feature equally good information. For example,, try Cornell Law School's **Legal Information Institute** Web site (**http://www.law.cornell.edu**). It is a wonderful, ad free, way to access the federal and state law on the Web. LII primarily links to 3rd party Web sites, including plenty of government sites, but it also has some of its own easily searchable content, primarily federal and New York law.

GOVERNMENT SEARCHING

21. Government Information Portals

The Federal government has a couple of sites that have pulled together the vast government resources available on the Web.

FirstGov (**http://www.firstgov.gov**) claims to be your fist stop in accessing federal and state government information. Set up like Yahoo! and other directories, it makes it easy to search or browse your way to government information.

Regulations.gov (**http://www.regulations.gov**) gives you one-stop shopping for commenting on proposed federal regulations.

22. Thomas from the Library of Congress

Thomas (**http://thomas.loc.gov**) is a creation of the Library of Congress in the spirit of Thomas Jefferson. It has an amazing collection of legislative information including bill summaries, roll call votes and committee reports. While there, check out the online exhibitions of the **Library of Congress** (**http://www.loc.gov/exhibits**)—amazing stuff.

23. Individual Agency Sites

Don't forget to search individual state and federal agency Web sites, which are generally bursting with useful information. Examples include:

- The **Internal Revenue Service** (**http://www.irs.gov**) has most of its forms online.
- **EDGAR** (**http://www.sec.gov/edgar.shtml**), the popular and newly revised Web site of the SEC.
- For a simple and complete list of federal government agencies, visit the **White House** agency list at (**http://www.whitehouse.gov/ government/independent-agencies.html**).

OTHER TIPS

24. Keep up with Legal Technology

Are you curious about the latest and greatest technology being used in legal offices all over the country? Interested on whether sole practitioners are having good luck with particular software? Curious as to whether it is worth buying an upgrade to a product you are already using? Look no farther than **Technolawyer** (**http://www.technolawyer.com**). It is a highly moderated listserv that keeps you in contact with what is really happening with legal offices and technology.

25. Use an RSS Reader

Web sites that change on a regular basis often have an RSS feed available. It is basically a way to have new information sent to you rather than you having to find it.

- **15 Minute RSS Tutorial** on how to use RSS and why you would want to do so from the Free Range Librarian (**http://frl.bluehighways. com/frlarchives/000123.html**).
- The tutorial features **Bloglines** (**http://www.bloglines.com**), a really easy to use RSS Reader. You can also use Outlook 2007 to manage your RSS feeds (**http://office.microsoft.com/en-us/ help/FX100340981033.aspx**).
- A list of law related RSS Feeds from Virtual Chase (**http://www. virtualchase.com/topics/rss_law.shtml**).

Glossary

A

act *see* statute.

administrative agencies part of the executive branch, administrative agencies have the role of being experts in and advising on a particular area.

ALR (American Law Reports) a secondary source of legal information that has case-specific information.

B

bar journal legal periodical aimed at the practicing attorney.

bill tracking following the process of legislation as it moves from its original proposal through committees to potential passing and signing by the executive.

Bluebook, a uniform system of citation style guide with a uniform system of citation. A small book with a blue cover, the *Bluebook* is used by most legal professionals for proper citation format.

boolean operator special word used to connect search terms when searching a database.

browsing looking through ordered lists of information, generally arranged hierarchically, to find information you want. One might browse a table of contents or a subject area of directory.

C

case law interpretation of statutory and regulatory law by the judicial branch.

citation abbreviated method of referring to a source of information. Found in both legal and non-legal documents, citations follow a specific format. In legal writing, the main resource for legal citation format is the *Bluebook*.

cite checking *see* Shepardizing.

code *see* statute.

codification process of organizing laws according to subject.

connector *see* boolean operator.

D

database organized collection of information, searchable by keyword.

default operator boolean operator (usually OR) that a database automatically chooses when no Boolean operator is selected.

defendant party who is being sued at the trial court level.

E

electronic research looking for answers to questions by using computer databases of information.

et seq Latin phrase meaning *all the following sections.* Statutory citations often use this phrase where the first section of the statute is cited and the rest are included.

F

Federal Register daily publication issued by the Government Printing Office that includes, among other things, notices on rule making.

field restricted search in Westlaw, a search of specific portions of a document like the title, author, parties, etc.

Five Questions a research strategy.

G

guidance information an administrative agency gives to help the regulated community comply with regulations.

H

hornbook textbook-like, in-depth, and detailed exploration of a broad legal topic like torts or contracts.

I

Internet also known as the Net. A collection of linked computers that lets users review and exchange information. The Internet includes features like e-mail, tel-net, bulletin boards, instant messaging, and the World Wide Web.

Internet service provider also known as an ISP. The company that gives you access to the Internet, your on-ramp to the information superhighway. ISPs facilitate your ability to dial up the Internet through a modem or have constant access to the Internet via fast Internet connections.

issue statement legal question that research aims to answer.

J

jurisdiction as referred to in this text indicates whether a regulation falls under state or federal law.

K

keyword term selected to find relevant documents in a database.

L

law review article article from a legal journal. Law reviews are generally based on detailed research and often focus on specialized topics. They help the researcher to find in-depth research on detailed topics.

legal dictionary resource for word definitions. Legal dictionaries are an excellent starting point for research.

legal encyclopedia secondary source with brief explanations of legal terms and concepts, often accompanied by references to relevant cases.

legislative history documentation of the process that a bill went through to become a law. Often used to interpret the law after its passage.

N

natural language searching querying a database using the same language that you would use to question a person, without using Boolean operators.

O

on point law that specifically addresses some or all of a particular issue.

P

paid legal database legal database that you can access only by subscribing or paying by the use.

parallel citation second location for the same case. For example, a case might be found both in a state reporter and the regional reporter.

phrase search searching a database for an exact phrase, with the search terms right next to each other. Quotation marks or parentheses often surround the phrase.

plaintiff person who sues at the trial court level.

practice book legal reference intended for use by the practicing attorney. Often in a three-ring binder, the practice book is meant to be a current reference on everything relevant to its specific subject area.

proximity search search of a database for terms close to each other, usually within 10 to 25 words of each other. This is often indicated with the Boolean operator NEAR.

Q

query request to a database for information it contains, using keywords joined by connectors.

R

regulated community businesses and individuals subject to an agency's regulations.

regulation also known as a rule. Laws created by administrative agencies to implement statutes. A regulation must have statutory authority granted by the legislature.

research looking through information to find the answer to a question.

research strategy plan created to make the researcher think about the research to be done, which thus makes the process more effective. The plan usually includes a determination of relevant law and the best keywords.

restatement textbook-like exploration of a single legal subject like torts, property or evidence.

rule *see* regulation.

rule-making process of creating a rule or regulation. The Administrative Procedures Act (APA) sets out the multi-step process at the federal level.

S

search directory search tool that breaks sites into categories to facilitate browsing.

search engine tool that lets you search through information on the Internet.

secondary sources sources of legal information designed to give you background information and lead you to primary law.

segment searching in Lexis, a search of specific portions of a document, such as the title, author, parties, etc.

shepardizing generally, the process of checking a law to make sure that it still applies. When Shepardizing cases, you may find other relevant cases that refer to your case, making Shepardizing a good research tool.

specialty search tools search engines and directories dedicated to specific topics like law or medicine.

statute also known as an act or code. A law created by the legislative branch of government.

stemming process in which a database automatically looks for common variations of a word, most commonly its plural form.

stopwords words that search tools ignore because they appear too frequently. Examples include the words *the*, *of*, and *a*.

T

table of contents like a book's table of contents, this search feature lets you see what sections of the law are available and easily access those sections.

terms and connectors used in Lexis to indicate Boolean search operators.

W

wildcard operator symbol used to find variations of a term. Sometimes called a root expander.

World Wide Web also known as www or the Web. A collection of computers that enables users to access information through an appealing graphical interface. It lets Web sites have images, colors, and other interesting features, rather than just plain text.

Index

A

act. *See* statutes
administrative agencies, 104
agency name, finding regulation, 108
American Jurisprudence, 145
American Law Reports (ALR), 144, 145
AND operator. *See* Boolean operators
asterisk (*), 11, 14, 37, 38, 41, 42

B

Ballentine's Law Dictionary, 145
bar journal, 147
bill tracking tools, 36, 37
Black's Law Dictionary, 145
Bluebook, 125
Boole, George, 4
Boolean operators, 4–6
  AND, 5–6, 14
  Casemaker, 41
  Lexis, 37
  Loislaw, 40
  NOT, 6, 14
  OR, 5, 14
  query formation, 24, 26
  Westlaw, 36
Boolean searching, 4, 17
browsing, 60, 83, 86–87
businesses, Web sites for, 67

C

case law, 124
  abbreviation format, 126t
  review of, 124
  search strategy, 124–133
    citation, 125–127
    party names, 127–131
    topic, 131
Casemaker, 41–42
  Boolean operators, 42
  case law
    abbreviation format, 126t
    citation, 125
    party names, 128–129, 130t
    topic, 132
  dictionaries and encyclopedias, 145
  explanatory sources, 152
  legal news, 153
  news sources, 153
  paid legal database comparison, 50t
  phrase search, 42
  proximity search, 42
  regulation, find by citation, 106
  statutes, find by
    citation, 86
    title, 90
  stemming, 42
  Table of Contents, 41, 108
  Thesaurus Expansion, 42

C (continued)

certiorari, 127
citation, finding with
  case law, 125–127
  regulation, 104–107
  search, 46
  statute, 84–88
cite check. *See* Shepardizing
civil law, 18
civil procedure, 18
code. *See* statutes
Code of Federal Regulation (CFR), 104
codification, 104
commercial law, 18
connectors. *See* Boolean operators
continuing legal education (CLE), 152
contract law, 18
Cornell Law School (Legal Information Institute), 87, 129, 132
  case law, abbreviation format, 126t, 130t–131t
court system, 124
crawlers. *See* spiders
criminal law, 18

D

database, 4, 24–27
  default operator, 5
defendant, 127
dictionary, legal, 20, 145

193